the**UNBREAKABLE**
Human Spirit

Randy Gonzales Jr.

More Heart Than Talent Publishing, Inc.

6507 Pacific Ave #329
Stockton, CA 95207 USA
Toll Free: 800-208-2260
www.MoreHeartThanTalentPublishing.com

FAX: 209-467-3260

Cover art by FlowMotion Inc.

I dedicate this book to _____
for the *SOUL* purpose of pursing greatness. The "Law Of Attraction" brought us together. As an advocate of lifelong learning, I support your vision for a better, brighter world. Through developing our "Unbreakable Human Spirits," we are prosperous in all aspects of life. I am blessed to have presented this book to you.

So, on this day _____, _____, 20_____, I am recognizing your will and passion to succeed. Your ability to lead by unwavering, applied faith and your decision to teach abundance by the examples you set are being noticed. You are a leader because of these actions. I'm proud to say that it's an honor and privilege to be surrounded by you.

If you gave me a dollar and I gave you a dollar, we both would have a dollar. But if I gave you an idea and you gave me an idea, we would both have two ideas. Let's take our ideas, fill them with joy, passion, and action, learn from each other, and impact the world one story at a time!

Your friend and
fellow networker,

_____

TABLE OF CONTENTS

FOREWORD BY JEFFERY COMBS
FOREWORD BY JEFFERY COMBS

It is my absolute privilege to be asked to write a foreword to Randy Gonzales' new book *The Unbreakable Human Spirit*. I met Randy several years ago when his spirit was being tested. At the time of our first meeting Randy did not own a car, lived in a spare bedroom with his sister and was financially challenged. At that point in Randy's entrepreneurial career he had every reason to be a victim. A victim he definitely was not, as I could tell there was a unique quality about him: a shine, a sparkle, a charisma that was infectious. I was able to witness a transformation in Randy that is rare in our society today. He began to attend my workshops, seminars, and events and a team of young people began to follow him. He transformed from being a leader to a leader-grower in a short period of time. His insight and wisdom about what he has been through is definitely the reason you deserve to read this book and pass it on to others. *The Unbreakable Human Spirit* is a book that every person who seeks to become more and deserve more will benefit from. Randy is an example of what it means to have "More Heart than Talent."

A WORD FROM THE AUTHOR

A WORD FROM THE AUTHOR

FOR OVER A DECADE I've marveled over the heart, mentality, and spirit of true legends. They have contributed incredible triumphs to the masses, separating themselves from good to great. Many of them left an eternal mark on this place called earth in the short journey we call life.

What I perceive as true brilliance is the discovery of one's true self, tested by the laws of nature and defined as one's greatest moments. It is in these moments that lives are changed forever. It is in these moments that we ultimately define who we really are and who we were destined to be.

This book contains examples of legends with a willingness to succeed. This is how fortunes are made and how lives are changed forever.

This is not a book about common people, nor do I intend my students or readers to consider their lives and futures to be common either. This book contains many secrets that only a few have discovered. But the few that stepped out and utilizing applied, unwavering faith as a result will never be forgotten. This is why I refer to them as "legends." You will learn more about them in later chapters.

Be prepared to take massive, fulfilling action as you discover that many of your own thoughts and desires are no different than those described in this book. Holding *The Unbreakable Human Spirit* in your hands, at this point in your life, is no surprise; it is no accident. The fact that we are meeting through this book, sharing our thoughts and realizing our dreams together, will absolutely develop your own unbreakable human spirit. So I dedicate this book to YOU!

1  BRILLIANCE UNFOLDED

Let's go out and shock the world, team! Together we can make a difference! Give it your best shot! Do today what others won't do so you can have tomorrow what others won't have! Whatever you do, do it with all your power, all your heart, and all your might! And remember, the man or woman who makes no mistakes doesn't usually make anything!

Brilliant people have brilliant thoughts, habits, and actions. The extraordinary people that brilliantly developed all of the above sayings tapped into their own unbreakable brilliance.

So how do you define brilliance? I define it as matured faith. I realized that the more successful one becomes, the more powerful one's mind grows in utilizing the unlimited power and strength of their own unbreakable faith. Every form that we take, we first unfold. Our minds, hearts, and souls render the thoughts of possibility, followed by our definite major purpose realized by our outcomes.

Not every step in faith has the desired outcome we expect. Some steps are designed for us as a life lesson. Faith when used grows, just like our muscles. When not

used, faith weakens. When neglected, it disintegrates.

When I give this valuable information to my students or clients in the form of lessons and trainings, ordinary people say, "I know this stuff already." But extraordinary people tell me it solidifies their beliefs about the intertwining circles between faith and brilliance and how they go hand in hand.

It reminds me of the words of that old song by Frank Sinatra: "Love and marriage go together like a horse and carriage." Ah yes, the sweet sound of the love and marriage between faith and brilliance. What a pair!

Here's some food for thought. When you think you know it all, you die. When you exercise your brilliance, you live. For the most part, most people get through life without ever really living. They don't exercise their possibility muscles.

Let me give you some advice early on that one of my mentors gave me many years ago. If you think you know it all, you don't. If you think it is impossible, it isn't, and if you think you are alone, you're not. Our thoughts are vibrations. Your subconscious is the gatekeeper of any thought. It will block out or let in whatever you have programmed it to do. It can't tell the difference between a penny and a dollar but will act upon your thoughts of hopelessness or possibility based upon your focus. So whatever you focus your mind on, that's where your mind

will be directed.

For example, what thoughts, dreams, or desires have you have had in your heart that you felt defeated over, or that maybe your soul felt ashamed about? In other words, times when you quit, threw in the towel, or didn't give it your all. Can you recall any? Of course you can. Now what type of thoughts are you feeling as you reminisce on these past failures? Wow! It's funny how quickly you can go from energy up to energy down by a single thought.

Ordinary people base their thoughts on concrete evidence. They lack the ability to utilize applied faith, which I will be covering in the next chapter. However, brilliant people base their thoughts on, "How can I?" They are fueled by possibility. It is the extraordinary people that raise their standards for the betterment of themselves and others who attain their desired outcome.

It's the extraordinary people who invented the lightbulb, developed the automobile, created heavy machinery to fly through the air with ease, and perfected a simple chicken recipe that is now known throughout the world. I'm sure the more you read, the more you will fully understand that you are not that much different than these great people. It's only that your thoughts may currently be different. Yes, I said *currently*. And why do you think I said currently? Can you improve? The answer: Yes. The full answer: Always. This is why you are where you're at—always. This is why you get paid exactly according to your worth—always. This

is why you attract the people and situations to you throughout your life, both good and bad—always.

When you unfold your true brilliance, the real you, the person you were meant to be, comes out soaring. Every one of us has the ability to become more than we thought we could be. Now together, let's see how our emotions run when we have a positive mental attitude versus a negative mental attitude.

For example, say to yourself, "I can't ever be rich, happy, or even fulfilled. I wasn't meant to be someone great. I stink at everything. I can't ever get anyone to listen to me. All my friends and family are broke—that's probably why I'm broke. Nobody likes me; therefore nobody will listen to me. I'm afraid. I'm afraid. I'm afraid."

How does that make you feel? Pretty disempowered! Maybe even crummy. Well, it was supposed to! Remember, it was just an exercise. Now, if you believe you're worthless, your body will actually start to shut itself down. You will age much more quickly due to stress and fear. Well, believe it or not, congratulations! You're using your faith muscles. But *how* you use your faith muscles is even more important than not using them at all. Let's see how having a positive mental attitude will increase your feelings of self worth and therefore raise your heart rate and provide more blood flow and energy to your body. Start by reading this:

"I am an extraordinary individual whose thoughts, actions, and visions have attracted the right people to

my life for the fulfillment of my greatest experiences. I'm tapping into my unbreakable brilliance, and my heart and faith will lead me to the answers that I am seeking with a burning desire."

Wow, say it out loud once more.

It might sound funny, and you probably don't normally talk like this, but what if you did? And what if for a small second you registered a spark of opportunity, a thought of possibility in your subconscious mind, the place where your brilliance grew up and still lives today? In other words, you want to excite your brilliance. You want to turn it on, baby!

Crack open a door of possibility or a window of hope in your subconscious and watch your brilliance serenade your ideas. Now, I don't know if there will be a candlelit dinner by the fireplace or some romantic music. But use your imagination… because this is exactly what you must understand in order to fully see the power of your true brilliance once ignited.

Because fate stands in the pathway of our ultimate destiny, we sometimes question where our heart really lies. Our heart acts as a shield that protects our most precious commodity—our soul. It serves as an ambassador to our faith. It is what we live for. It is what brilliant individuals, including the many people I've interviewed and taught, are willing to die for. It becomes their unbreakable destiny powered by their unbreakable human spirit!

The paths that I'm speaking of are so close together; they are separated only by a single decision. However, the end results are dramatically different. These are the paths that only our ultimate destiny will allow through, the paths that only true champions in life will ever cross. The meaning we give to things relies solely on our beliefs as we travel each path, shielded by our heart of destiny, encouraged by our ambassadors, and solidified by our unbreakable faith.

The "death of all things" must be our declaration regarding our decisions—meaning we have no other options available. What is a decision? I believe a decision is your ultimate power! The opposite of decision is procrastination.

Procrastination is the greatest thief of time. And what do thieves do? Do they empower or disempower? Do they serve you or do you a disservice? If you've ever had anything stolen from you, you probably experienced a sense of discomfort or a feeling of violation. It's exactly the same with your human spirit.

If you give in to procrastination, be prepared to have an unfulfilling life. Period! No ifs, ands, or buts! Procrastination will suck the wind right out of you. Your spirit, heart, soul, health, and finances will constantly take direct hits with no protection if you allow this to happen.

I like to think of procrastination as a poison. Yes, it's that extreme. When you place importance on something,

you automatically give a higher priority than other areas. So why do we procrastinate? Why do we allow something to steal our dreams like a thief in the night?

One word—the mother of achieving all massive fulfilling dreams—"action," and the antidote to destiny's purifier: "my actions"! You will never get to meet your true brilliance if you can't create a decision, driven by massive, fulfilling action!

Closing a chapter in your external book is nothing more than living with fulfillment. This opens new possibilities for hope and greatness throughout your life. Peace of mind comes into effect. Greater abundance starts to flow in your direction. You now have the ability to start leaving with ease.

Deep in the valley of opportunity lie our greatest moments. This valley is a humble place where emotions run high and spirits run free. It's a place where standards are set and influenced. It's a place where the word "miracle" was conceived by the mother of persistence and the father of laser focus.

Usually, when we reach the top of any achievement the world cheers us on and rewards us for our ability to proceed through our decisions. But to whom do we turn to when our journey starts out rocky from below and our hearts are tested? When the odds tell us, "Not in this lifetime, buddy!" When life tells us, "It's too risky! Better go back to what you know you... You won't get any fulfillment out

of, but it's safe." What gives us fulfillment when all the possibilities are locked in the palm of our hands, waiting to break free of restraints? The answer... our disciplines!

While at times discipline may seem very painful, it can also be very rewarding. There are two types of pain we will experience in life: the pain of discipline, or the pain of regret. Discipline weighs ounces, while regret weighs tons.

Pay particular attention to this section. It is so crucial for you to understand the difference between living a life you deserve and living a life of regret. The "I wish I would have"—or going through life using the "keeping your fingers crossed" theory is not a fulfilling approach.

Making decisions takes massive, immediate action. It requires leading with your heart and not your head, even when you're not ready. Where you are, whether you are sitting down or standing up, doesn't matter. Wherever you're at is a good point to start.

When you are able to recognize these moments and decide on your ultimate outcome with an attitude of "whatever it takes," then and only then will you enter a place of brilliance. Failure is not an option. Take off the blinders of doubt and watch the true beauty you have unfold.

Brilliance attracts people like Thomas Edison, Henry Ford, Colonel Sanders, Michael Jordan, Abraham Lincoln,

Mahatma Gandhi, the astronauts of Apollo 13, and one of my great phenomenal legends, Jesus Christ. (So far, he has about sixty-five percent of the population on his team—I find that fascinating!)

Based on my philosophy, these are true legends that have journeyed to a place many people have shied away from. It's a place where their true, unbreakable human spirit was challenged by unearthly fire and torment. Through developing their own unbreakable human spirit, these incredible humans experienced the joy of tapping into our ultimate destination while on earth: our true brilliance.

Every moment of every day, we are given an opportunity to rise above the rest. Every day we open our eyes is a day closer to our destiny's moment of glory. Every day that challenges arise gives us hope for opportunities for greatness to appear just in the nick of time, utilized by the power and execution of applied faith.

At times, you might feel a sense of inadequacy. The questions start to boggle your mind. "Can I really do it? Do I really have what it takes?" Whatever it may be—a business idea, a mate of choice—the possibilities are endless. It's important to fully understand the principals of brilliance. I hope you understand how important it is for your personal development to know how to utilize the power of applied, unwavering faith. To walk by applied, unwavering faith and not by sight is truly brilliance unfolded.

On Sundays when I was growing up, I attended Sunday school. We would always talk about the power of faith. We used to sing a song in Sunday school—the words went like this, "Faith, faith, faith; just a little bit of faith, faith, faith, faith; just a little bit of faith, you don't need a whole lot, just use what you got; faith, faith, faith; just a little bit of faith." So I did!

What is faith? Can we see it? Can we touch it? Can we hear it? The answer to all of these questions may shock you: Yes! Yes! Absolutely, unequivocably YES! When your unbreakable human spirit is first tested, your mind goes on "autopilot." In other words, whatever you feed your subconscious will fuel your body. Faith is simply the ability to recognize opportunity and capitalize on it with action. Several of my early mentors called this type of faith "applied faith," or the action behind faith.

What is the difference, you may ask? *Applied* means to take action, to use, to take initiative. It makes no difference whether you are looking for a spouse, the car or home of your dreams, or even a business venture. You must recognize the power of applied, unwavering faith,

which I like to call "borrowing from your dreams." If you are seeking a positive outcome, it's okay to look into your future, because that is where you will be spending the rest of your life! Your dreams are merely a glimpse of what could be.

Analyze your life. Look at the great attributes you possess. Look at your weaknesses and turn those weaknesses into your strengths. Take one hundred percent full responsibility for your life and your future.

I was talking with my mother one night about the ability to look into the future. The time was 8:13 p.m. I told her, "Mom, it doesn't matter how hard you try, there is absolutely nothing you can do about yesterday. To be even more specific, Mom, there is absolutely nothing you can do about earlier today. To be totally truthful, there is absolutely nothing you can do about 8:12 p.m. tonight, and that was just a minute ago.

"I know it's 8:13 p.m., but brilliant people understand that you can do something about 8:14 p.m. tonight. And if that's the case, then you can do something about 8:15 p.m. and 8:30 p.m.

"To move into your brilliance, it's even more important to understand this: yesterday is history and tomorrow is a mystery." My mom told me she had never thought of that, and she had a breakthrough.

Most people don't borrow from their future. Instead, they borrow from their past, and that's why they are stuck.

They remain in an area that already exists. I know this was the case for me earlier in my life. From the age of eighteen to about twenty-three, I constantly lived in the past. I remember telling myself, "I wasn't ever good enough. I never grew up with anybody wealthy. My parents were always negative. That's why I'm negative"— blah! Blah! BLAH!

I call this a "throw up party"! A lot of people I attracted to me had this same mentality. And after we finished our throw up sessions, we would try (try, as in not really going to happen) prospecting clients. It was a total mess and I couldn't figure out why.

Then it hit me like a ton of bricks! The laws! Just saying it still gives me chills... Understanding the laws and principals of success. Have you ever had the wind knocked out of you? Let me tell you, the sweetest breath is the very next one you take that says, "I'm still alive, and I'm going to make it!" Understanding these laws and principals are just like that next breath of fresh air. When you understand and apply them, you realize at that moment you will make it.

I want you to fully understand and engage in the power of borrowing from your dreams. You will develop peace of mind by constantly using this power, by simply applying it. Again, "applied" simply means taking action—unwavering action, meaning that you cannot be detoured in any other direction that your mind will not allow.

Finally, the keynote word is "faith," which is a belief, trust, or confidence that is not necessarily based on logic, facts, reason, or empirical data. Instead, faith is based on *volition*, which is often associated with a *transpersonal* relationship with a *higher power*, a *person*, elements of *nature*, and/or a perception of the *human race* as a whole. Wow! That was a mouthful, but understanding this is the power you possess to see the future.

Many years ago when I was first becoming an entrepreneur, I had nothing of financial significance. To make people laugh in those days, I used to tell a joke that I was so broke that if you looked up the singular word "broke" in the dictionary, you would find a picture of me there. And if you looked up the plural form of the word "broke" in the dictionary, you would see my family. And if you looked up the word "broke" in a thesaurus, you would see my friends and their families!

Imagine what kind of message I was sending to the universe. I didn't mean to offend any of my family or friends—I just wanted people to know that my greatest teachers didn't come from my bloodline or from my buddies from high school or my neighborhood.

I was done hearing excuses like, "What do you think, we're rich?" or "Do you think money grows on trees?" Or how about this one: "Put your want in one hand and crap in the other and see which fills faster!" What a poor mental attitude! If you are or planning to be a parent, here

are some words of advice: Always have a positive mental attitude.

Being brought up like that and growing up poor were my toughest challenges until I started to study the laws and principals of success. All of my family and friends growing up were poor mentally, physically, financially, and most importantly, spiritually. All I wanted, even as a child, was more so I could be more, so I could do more... so I could contribute more.

I remember crying to myself sometimes as a kid, not understanding why some kids at the public school I attended where so cruel to me. They made fun of me for not having the best clothes, for wearing hand-me-downs. I didn't understand—I used to like it as a kid when my relatives brought over some used clothes and shoes. They bought name brand stuff that my mother could not afford. To me it was a blessing. But deep in my heart I've always wanted more.

The more I wanted success, the more I hungered for it. The more my close friends and family members told me not to be such a dreamer, the bigger I dreamed. My passion for who I am today and who I was becoming back then was due to my ability to master applied, unwavering faith."

To this day, I utilize and exercise my ability to rely on my applied, unwavering faith. Remember—if you don't use it, you lose it. So I use mine as much as humanly

possible; it's how I choose to live my life. I teach my students and business partners alike to utilize it when they have an idea about any project. The importance of borrowing from your dreams may be the tipping point for many of you—it was the tipping point for me to achieve massive success in both my personal and professional endeavors.

Many of you will be able to relate to this. As I was building some of my businesses early on, I can remember going to do presentations with no car, no money, and sometimes no clue how I was going to eat that day—but by borrowing from my future, I would always see things as they would be, not as they were.

I *always* found a way to show my prospects my business plan. I knew that having incredible people join me spreading my vision would solidify my purpose and my practices.

It's funny thinking back on some of my early presentations. I would say that one out of twenty-five prospects would ask me what kind of car I drove back when I didn't own one. The power of my thoughts was my first taste of the law of attraction. It seemed that every time I thought to myself, "Please, Prospect, don't ask what car I drive," they WOULD!

With a big smile I would tell them that I was in the process of purchasing my dream car, which at the time was a Dodge Viper. That was all I told them. By doing this, I

expressed to them my vision and excitement.
(Of course, I would wait a while after they left, and then I would walk home to my apartment—the one that I couldn't afford.) But I knew I would have that very car someday if I just kept taking action. I didn't lie to my prospects. I just borrowed from my future—about three and a half years, to be exact.

In the meantime, I had to move into my buddy's garage. I had hit a low point. I believe at that point my Creator was testing me to see how much I really wanted to go after and pursue my destiny. I slept on the cold, concrete floor. Winters were cold and summers were hotter, especially at night. But knowing in my heart that I would fulfill my dreams in spite of the struggles I was attracting to my reality was all part of my process.

The universe gave me the ability to create a story that inspires others to keep going, even when close friends and family say it isn't going to work or it's ok to give up and be ordinary. If you follow that advice, your spirit will haunt you for the rest of your life for not believing in yourself. I'm so glad I took the road less traveled, and you will be too. I share portions of my journey not to discourage you, but to inspire you to borrow from your own future with an unbreakable passion that allows you to go after your dreams.

Today, I don't sleep on a concrete floor without a bed in my buddy's garage. I own a beautiful California king-

size bed. It has solid wooden posts on all four corners; it measures twenty-seven inches in diameter and stands over seven feet tall. It's a long way from that cracked cement floor full of spiders! My mattress is made of memory foam that molds to my body when I lay down to rest. I can assure you, my garage is not used for sleeping—it now houses not one but two of my dream cars. Yes, in my garage you'll find my gorgeous graphite metallic Dodge Viper along with a beautiful, shiny, pewter Cadillac Escalade. One for winter and one for summer, of course!

I was so passionate about owning a home, after not having one for so long. Now I have millions of dollars' worth of both homes and land. Currently I've been designing a 17,000 square-foot home I deserve to build on my land. I've always dreamed of doing a Weekend Warriors training in my own backyard, and now I'm making my dream come to fruition.

I'm in the process of obtaining my helicopter license for business and pleasure. By the time you read this, I will be in the process of realizing another one of my dreams—purchasing my own helicopter.

I'm not telling you these things to impress you; I'm telling you these things because I'm extremely proud of where I'm at in my life and where I'm going. More importantly, I'm proud of the people I get to inspire who choose to do the same. When your certainty far exceeds the world's doubt, the world will see your vision. A few years

ago, someone asked me if I had a chance to do it all over again, would I? My response was: "All I know is that I have one life to live, and if I live it correctly, once is enough."

What touches my soul are the stories of people who didn't give in to the ones that try ("try" meaning "not really going to happen") to steal their dreams. I feel very blessed that I have the ability to give back through my books, CDs, and trainings. This allows me to expand my team of elite thinkers who are full of passion and drive for one sole purpose: greatness. This team is handpicked—not every one is invited. I call this group my Millionaire Mastermind Roundtable. Together as a team, in unison, we go around the world connecting with the right individuals who are committed to taking these philosophies to higher levels by optimizing applied, unwavering faith powered by each of our own unbreakable human spirits.

My passion is to create, spread, and teach wealth and abundance to others. The reason I want every one of you to create millions is so that you can contribute from abundance versus scarcity. This will be known as one of the highest achievements of your lifetime, and for many of you, this is your ultimate destiny.

3  HEARTBREAKING DEFEAT

At any pinnacle in life we might encounter heartbreaking defeat. It's how we grow. It's how we expand. It's how we learn. It's how we develop. Bottom line, it's how we win! Problems are given to us in life to be solved. As human beings, we require them to grow.

In this process, any real winner will experience tears, tears, and more tears. But what are tears? They are the clashing of emotions—frustration versus perseverance. These emotions are at war with one another, and only one will be triumphant. The really extraordinary thing is that it's entirely up to you to decide which of these emotions will be the last one standing for you.

Many of us have cried when we won something of personal value. And many of us have also cried when we lost someone or something of personal value, such as a close friend or family member passing away. This is a natural part of our human makeup. It shows us what we value the most in life—each other. It shows us our own personal threshold.

When I was only nine years old, my parents went

through a bitter divorce. It was a very trying time for me. At that point, I felt as if I was split between love and hate. The only thing holding my world together was my relationship with my older sister Jennie.

When a child is put into a position of choosing sides, it can really have an effect on their ability to give and receive love. For me, the question was whether my father was right for leaving my mother, or whether my mother was right for wanting him to stay. At nine years old, I knew I should have been thinking of other things, but it was part of my destiny to understand how I could personally deal with this type of situation. Let me explain. As I grew up, I had the ability to connect with many other individuals who grew up in dysfunctional families. So today, I look at my own experience as a blessing.

Many people talk about their past and still live there. I truly believe that it is not your fault if you become a victim of any sort. It's only your fault if you remain one.

Attempting to make both parents happy was a difficult task. As I got older, I learned that their divorce was between them; it wasn't about me. I remember telling them that if they had anything negative to say about each other to please keep it to themselves because I didn't want to hear it. And they honored this.

Growing up with a poor mental attitude, always seeking love and acceptance, was no easy task. I use to think as a child, "How could something so simple be so complicated?"

Imagine what it does to a child's spirit when someone they love despises someone else they love. The child observes the physical and verbal abuse—but loves both parties equally.

All I can say twenty-two years later is that it was an outstanding lesson for me at the age of nine to start to develop my own unbreakable human spirit. It prepared me for my future and my destiny. Overcoming those heartbreaking challenges as a young boy allowed me to start believing in my purpose, which became assisting others to develop their own unbreakable human spirit regardless of their past and regardless of their present. As a child, I discovered that the only thing I could look towards was the future. So I did!

At this young age, I realized it wasn't my ideas that clashed. I wasn't the one with unfulfilling thoughts. If I had decided to hold all those feelings in my heart and soul as I aged, today I would probably be in an angry state of mind—or jail.

By utilizing my ability to turn heartbreaking defeat into opportunity, and opportunity into fulfilling success, I've now been able to empower tens of thousands of people. I know that before my time is up on earth, that number will increase to tens of millions of people through sharing my teaching, philosophies, and life experiences.

I believe in a team atmosphere and team development. I believe in team building as well as team celebrating. By

team, I simply mean: Together Each Achieves Miracles. And developing your own unbreakable human spirit is nothing short of a miracle.

You see, this book is really not about me. It's about *you* and your transformation! This just happens to be part of my story. The real story is how you can take this information, determine where you're at in life, and move forward from there in the direction you choose. That's why I dedicated this book to your empowerment.

I know there are many people who have experienced much worse things than I did, and they still made something valuable of their lives. You yourself might be reading this book because you are searching and open to the idea of personal development. And you are gaining power and strength by being surrounded by great thoughts and positive energy.

There is absolutely nothing you can do about your past. Yesterday is history. But there is absolutely something you can do now about tomorrow, if you choose—if you are open to receive a gift. Say this out loud—yes, out loud. Most of you will not do it, for whatever reason. But for those of you who are open and willing, tell the universe, "It's my time for greatness! It's my time for abundance! It's my time for peace of mind, and I will be the one to determine my destiny!"

Go back and reread this last section. Come on! You've thought of negative stuff in your life that didn't serve you;

now, try something positive. Go ahead—do it now! If you're brave enough to tell the universe what you deserve, then do it—take ownership!

You have the ability to think yourself into any endeavor, positive or negative. Your mind will allow you to think of possibilities and impossibilities based upon whatever you feed your subconscious. Your heart will be measured by the toughest of critics: YOU! Taking one hundred percent full responsibility is the only way to optimize your achievements.

Too many people like to point a finger at other people when certain problems arise. Be a leader and look at your hand when you're pointing at someone. Always note that three of those fingers are pointing back at *you*. Leaders understand this.

Today, start where you're at and give yourself the gift of enlightenment. Reflect on the passion you possess, not the heartbreaking moments in your life. Create a memory of the times you were proud of something you accomplished. When it's all said and done, your "once in a lifetime" won't be back again.

Take a chance—more importantly, place a sure bet on yourself! Your story of how you overcame heartbreaking moments will be very inspiring to others. Many people will read this book and learn from me. But I'm only one person. The real gift is the opportunity I have to learn from millions like you—the ones that stepped out and tapped into their

own brilliance; the ones that borrowed from their dreams when the odds were stacked against them; the ones who found a way after heartbreaking defeat. We all must accept challenges in order to grow spiritually, physically, and financially.

Like many of you, the challenges in my life did not stop at the age of ten, eleven, twelve, or thirty. There are continual opportunities to grow, and if we don't grow, we shrink! You can take that to the bank.

When I was a senior in high school, my sweetheart at the time and I realized that we were going become new parents by bringing a new life into this world. A baby! I was seventeen and she was eighteen. This was a *huge* inspiration for who I am today. Once again I had to realize that if I looked at what I was seeing with empowerment and not discouragement, it would catapult me through. And it did! My daughter Darion (who has just become a teenager) is learning to develop her own unbreakable human spirit. And she is learning to take our old days of poverty and teach her friends new ways of thinking—I love it!

So far, I've shared experiences from my personal life. But what about my business life? By the time I was twenty-four, I was a college dropout. I had been involved in seven failed businesses. I had accumulated over $90,000 in personal dept. My human spirit was challenged, and through this I learned the importance of developing it.

Going back to what I learned as a young boy, I believed

that I was special like many of the people I looked up to, no matter what other people thought of me. I learned to let go of disempowering beliefs and replace them with more empowering, fulfilling ones. All of the rewards I have today came with a price. This price came with lots of heartbreaking moments. But in time, without a doubt, my disappointments became opportunities for me to raise my standards.

I did lots of questioning about my own ability to think, love, prosper, and feed my subconscious with positive thoughts. For me, doing the things I did was a result of my positive mental attitude, telling myself, "I will do whatever my heart desires because I CAN!"

A failed relationship with my daughter's mom, getting two cars repossessed within one week of each other, becoming literally homeless—I experienced all of this. I rotated sleeping on the couches and floors of various friends and family members. I finally ended up in a friend's garage, sleeping on the concrete cement floor in a thin sleeping bag. I was afraid to tell anyone where I lived, because my goals and dreams were too big and too close to give up on. What I learned was that it was my own responsibility to manage my thoughts.

If you have recurring problems or negative situations, it is because of the law of attraction. You attract it. If you think you can, you can. If you think you can't, you can't. So think you can, and you will!

Leaders learn to focus on what could be instead of what is. During this process, each day I was challenged by my personal economics, as well as by friends telling me it was okay to give up and give in. When they told me I was just a big dreamer, my developing unbreakable human spirit would put all of its power and might into the passion and conviction to hold my backbone straight and my head up high. My spirit told me to stand on my own two feet and move forward by applied, unwavering faith—and to *never* give up. This inner voice told me, "I won't give up on you, so you better not give up on me. So stand your ground!" I knew when I listened I was closer than ever to achieving my dreams.

Within three years, my applied, unwavering faith paid off. The ability to realize your dreams is one of the sweetest, most breathtaking moments you will ever discover for yourself. This will happen for you too if your dreams and purpose are greater than any heartbreaking moments of defeat. So dream a big dream! And act on that dream, and you will discover as I have that the power of mastery is within your reach!

4  LAST ONE STANDING

Have you ever heard the term "rising star"? Have you ever wondered what it would feel like to shine in *your* moment of glory? This chapter is dedicated to all the people in the world who stood the test of time against all odds; they firmly stood their ground and were in fact the last one standing.

I remember attending a conference in Dallas, Texas, sitting among 25,000 people. Watching the leaders of the company receive recognition for their production, I was touched emotionally. I wondered in my heart if that could ever be me.

As a young father and a clueless entrepreneur, I knew if I kept searching and kept pushing through, I would see this light everybody else was seeing at the end of this tunnel I was supposedly in. For starters, I never knew I had to go through a tunnel to be fulfilled. But talking with many, many people, it seemed more and more that my ideas on business and success only sounded good to me.

Being laughed at, put down, and even mocked didn't make the process any easier. I wondered why I wasn't financially successful by the time I was twenty. The answer was simple.

I simply wasn't ready for the responsibilities that came along with success. So I made up my mind to find out what I was lacking. I discovered that a lot of baggage from my past had to be released. Not feeling good about myself was definitely holding me back. Learning to love myself first was a key ingredient to this receipe for achieving my dreams. This enabled me to stop being afraid of my results and to continue to thrive regardless of the outcome.

Until I was introduced to the "law of attraction," a lot of my actions did not make sense to me. It's one thing to be enthused on your journey, but you can also be enthused in the wrong direction. The law of attraction gave me the ability to understand that it was up to me to raise my standards if I wanted to attract different people than the ones in my life who were busy shooting down my dreams. I realized that my circle of influence played a key role in the outcome of my bank account. It's so true what many millionaires say about your circle of influence—you will act and react exactly like the people that surround you.

The venture I was involved with when I was eighteen years old lasted about two years. It was known as a startup, which simply meant a ground floor opportunity to me. The bigger the risk, the bigger the reward, right? It's funny how many of the ground floor opportunities I was involved in never got off the ground. Many people referred to these circumstances as casualties.

When I became successful, I said to myself, "Circumstances? Hell, I make circumstances!" And I have never seen a successful leader in any field that didn't feel the same way.

In each one of the companies I was striving to reach the top position, only to find myself alone. In one company, the owner didn't even attend the last convention when he knew the company was near its end.

I never understood the reason why people knocked startup companies or ideas, because that's where all the vision starts. I learned so much from each venture before I achieved success. Each one propelled me forward into a new venture. This process along with my childhood lessons strengthened my spirit. So when you come across a challenge, always say to yourself, "This will make a great story someday!"

Like anyone perusing a dream, I was filled with a vision to succeed. Along the way I was tested many times. My heart was striving for success, but my body was crying failure.

So many mixed emotions would go through my brain everyday before I started to condition my mind for success. I will never hesitate to thank my Creator every chance I get for giving me such a big heart. Like my good friend Jeffery Combs says, "More heart than talent." Every time I hear that phrase, I think to myself that it was intended for me. Every time I hear it, I definitely know it is not meant

only for me, but for millions of others with a passion for greatness. Deep down I know having a greater purpose is what successful people spend their energy on. It's why we live.

I was clueless in the beginning on how to develop myself. I just knew I must do it. I didn't quite know how; I just knew it was important. Personal development simply means developing yourself from the inside out. Your human spirit can be broken if you don't allow it to develop. You must allow yourself to grow. More importantly, you must give yourself permission to grow. Let yourself know that it's okay to fail—it's how you learn and grow. Problems are our greatest moments if we don't settle for the outcome. Our only solution lies in the direction that faith leads.

If your faith is anchored in scarcity, it will only fuel your problems. If your faith comes from abundance, then you have at your fingertips a vast array of solutions to any problem. That's where you gain power. You deserve to live a fulfilling life of peace, happiness, and prosperity. Without going the extra mile, we could never discover new talents that we possess. Without giving it our all, we will never fulfill our destiny.

I found my calling at the young age of nine. My purpose became developing myself through my spirit's resilience. I knew I was meant to enlighten and empower others. My purpose still is to explore greatness and achievement. These are the steps up the staircase to your dreams. They

direct you to go from good to outstanding.

Outstanding literally means that you stand out. Now, I don't know if this is a word or not, but I've seen thousands of brilliant people that are "in-standing," meaning that they don't take risks; they don't tap into their brilliance. They have tremendous ideas, but they never *act* on them! Therefore they just stand—or as I like to put it, *in-stand*. They don't raise their hand when life calls their name for greatness, so they never get recognized for what they possess. I use to think, "No risk, no reward," but today I truly believe, "No action, no reward." Simple, I know, but not easy!

Let me tell you firsthand that being the last one standing comes with a price, a price deep in your soul that cannot be ignored. Whether you pay this price or not, your human spirit will never forget.

I thank my Creator every chance I get for giving me and the other incredible people that surround me such an enormous hearts. Without a big heart, I couldn't live a fulfilled life. With it, I know the people I come in contact can evolve into the men or women they were destined to be. Set your standards high! That way, if you fall, you realize you're not flat on the ground—you may just be sitting up! Have fun with your goals. Experience every great thing in life that you can.

Optimization is the ability to recognize opportunity and use it to highest degree of mankind. When I speak

about optimization, many eyes open up and start to glaze over. I see the lightbulbs go on, beginning to generate thoughts of new ideas and possibilities. If you find yourself in this place, come back to me for just a minute, and then I'll set you loose.

There are NO DISCOUNTS at the checkout counter of success. You must be willing to pay full price, or else you cannot claim what is rightfully yours by divine right. Let me ask you this, have you ever been let down? Of course you have. It's a human emotion to feel let down. Have you ever given love and not received it in return? Again, of course you have. Most people I've coached would say that it is tragic when something like that happens. But by developing a positive mental attitude, you realize that just having the ability to give love, even when it is not returned, is still a gift. Why? Because you have the ability to love; it's an emotion.

Understand this! Everything we do and everything we become can be directly related to an emotion our subconscious gives to our conscious. We call it a surprise. Do you likes surprises? Most people do. But actually, you like the good one! The bad ones we call problems—not surprises. However, we require problems, because it's how we grow. It's how we evolve. Problems are given to us to be solved. Everything you have today was once a problem—your shoes, your car, the plane you flew in, the e-mail you just sent, the phone you talked on today.

If nobody wanted to solve problems, you wouldn't have the luxuries you have today, and our society would perish.

So accept your challenges. They are your chance to give back and contribute to life. Some of life's greatest gifts are opportunities (better known as "problems"). These so-called problems are given to you because you attracted them, and life knew you could come up with a perfect solution.

And when you call out to your human spirit for guidance, it illuminates the way. This gives you the ability to teach others how to grow from their experiences. Isn't that amazing?

Take a minute to look around you and see all the opportunities we have created. The ability to drive a car is a pretty incredible solution. Maybe you have a teleconference line—that is an amazing solution. Maybe you have had a loved one who was hooked up to a breathing machine to help them breathe. Maybe you know of an infant that was born premature, and as a result this machine allowed that baby to develop their lungs so someday they could live a normal life. Maybe someone you know is living today because of a heart, lung, or kidney transplant. To find solutions for the betterment of mankind is truly one of life's great rewards.

Showing gratitude for the things you have will only allow you to accept more from life's catalog of choices.

45

Wow! When you go home, by the click of a button your remote garage door opens up with a light on so you can see inside the garage when it's dark outside, and it closes by another click of a button when you are safely inside. Truly amazing!

We must form habits to be the last one standing. Winners develop habits that losers shy away from. Creating the habit of fulfilling action will pay you way beyond the price it costs you. When you develop your own unbreakable human spirit, you experience life's greatest gift: fulfillment.

5   PERSISTENCE

I call persistence the father of all achievement. Find any leader of any major organization, and you will see persistence written all over his or her face. Ask anyone who has achieved anything great in life what they did to achieve that greatness, and they'll tell you they persisted beyond the norm. In other words, they kept on keeping on!

After experiencing a heartbreaking defeat, your real moment of truth emerges. In high school, my football coach used to say, "Now is the time to separate the men from the boys." He gave us the chance to dig deep, to really see what we were made of. When we felt whipped, he would yell out, "Fourth quarter! Fourth quarter!" which simply meant that the winner of the game would be decided by whoever showed the most heart. He would say, "I don't care if you're beat, tired, or wasted. I don't care if they are bigger, stronger, or smarter than you—the one with the most heart will take home the victory." As a result, that year our record was 8-0—not bad for being laughed at for the previous year's record of 1-7.

As a team, we persisted regardless of what the newspapers, friends, and other schools said. Our coach told us there was nothing we could do about the past. We

could only set the pace for the future if we worked harder than anybody else, with persistence. We knew if the bigger, stronger teams worked out for an hour, we had to work out for two hours. If that team conditioned for forty-five minutes straight, we conditioned for ninety minutes straight.

Even though we were not supposed to take our equipment home, about three-fourths of the team snuck their gear home just so they could practice on the weekends. And when game time came, we knew it was time to play. So we did!

Going the extra mile is a key factor when you are developing yourself in any endeavor. Whether it's a sport, an idea, or a relationship, as a leader you must be willing to go the extra mile. This is how you develop your persistency muscle. Your habits become second nature. At that point, you develop the heart of a champion.

As my personal coach used to say, "Persistence is what separates the winners from the winers; the champs from the chumps." We must learn to be good winners as well as good losers. Nothing is worse than a poor loser or a poor winner. Be grateful for your ability to be persistent.

I believe that if you could turn your life-alternating moment into a cartoon, I would describe it something like this: The journey of an achiever's success depends upon the road you take. On one side, you have the road of ease and certainty. And on the other side is the road

of possibility and uncertainty. Right in the middle is a green sign saying, "Persistence is the father of achievement." Behind this sign is an old wooden post mounted in the ground. Under the green back frame, a white spinning pointer allows you to choose your destiny. Persistence has a major effect on your destiny, which I like to call your outcome. What you do is place your finger towards the direction you want to go... and away you go! This is not a game of chance where you spin the pointer and say, "Life is taking me that way, so that's where I guess I'd better go." No—*you* point the pointer in the direction where you *choose* to go, letting the world know exactly where you're headed so there will be no mistake about how you end up where your do. You don't need to tell anybody but yourself: "I got here because I chose to be here."

Persistence comes with a few key factors: accountability, responsibility, and action. Regardless of unforeseen circumstances, you must approach every step of the way with a willingness to succeed on the road that lies ahead of you.

If you could go to this crossroad, which road would you take? Would you choose the road of least resistance, or would you set the pace? This is a great question to ask yourself if you really want to see if you're a true leader.

Here is a simple tip if you want to know how to be a leader: Lead! Leaders lead! They lead by example. They lead by innovation. And most importantly, when the boats starts rocking and the waves start crashing, leaders stand up straight, set sail, and move forward.

Most people in the world like to tell people what to do rather than lead by example; we call them managers. Leaders leave a trail for others to follow. They tend to get lots of respect, and they also tend to have more heartbreaking moments. But they also get reward beyond compare.

Leaders are the pioneers of every thriving industry. They attain the unbreakable status of legends. You see, leaders are highly motivated. If something doesn't work, they start asking intelligent questions. Questions like, "Why didn't it work?" "How can I improve it?" A lot of successful legends keep accurate data of their progress. They know exactly where they're at. They fully understand that when their why is big enough, and that little gutter rat of opposition comes knocking, persistence came talking.

They adhere to the attitude that failure is not an option. They stand by their promise to themselves to never give up or give in. They live every nanosecond with precision. They develop total encompassing gratitude for what they have. They are the biggest givers in life. As a result, they end up being the biggest receivers. Giving and receiving go hand in hand. You can't have one without the other. Persistence is the heart in the phrase "more heart than talent."

I'd rather have three people with heart than a thousand with talent. Heart will always beat out talent. Your life was meant to experience the possibility of wonder realized by perseverance. When you grow a tree, you must first plant a seed. As you water it, with adequate sunlight it will grow. If it is a fruit tree, it will harvest fruit. Of course, some of the fruit will be lost to birds or insects, but that's all relative to the circle of life. When you arrive at the place of certainty, you'll always allow other people to find ways to improve their lives by what you've done. It's how we all grow.

What you will find is that there is plenty for everyone. We live in such an abundant world. Some of the people who have inspired me to be an innovator and tap into my creative thought process—where my persistence evolves daily into passion—were people like Thomas Edison, Henry Ford, and the Wright Brothers, to name a few. Let me tell you why.

The mastery of persistence goes to Thomas Edison. In my own journey when I'm faced with opposition, I think to myself, "What would Edison do?" and I keep moving forward. He was a true great innovator in his time, and a lot of his innovations still live on today—the incandescent lightbulb, for instance.

Do you really know how he created the lightbulb? Let me tell you. He actually didn't invent it. The idea of the lightbulb was around for many years before Edison. He

just brought a couple of old ideas together, and *bang!*

…Well, there was actually a little more to it than that. Let me explain. With his incredible persistence and the ability to track his progress, he came to a conclusion. During one of his catnaps, his subconscious went to work. After 10,000-plus experiments, his idea had finally arrived. Through creative vision and the law of compensation, Edison saw the purpose of his brains and the ideas of his soul. These ideas that Edison had derived were nothing new to anyone—they were made up of old ideas that he put together.

One of his ideas was that if you can take a wire and apply electrical friction to that wire, it would become so hot that it would create a light. A lot of people found that out way before Edison's time. That wasn't the problem. The problem Edison faced was how to control the wire so that when it gathered all that light from the heat source, it wouldn't burn up.

He tried a few experiments. I'm joking; it was more in the range of 10,000-plus as I mentioned earlier! The best part is, none of them worked. Talk about persistence! At this point, he had had it. He knew he had done everything possible he could do with his conscious mind, and so he rested. As he rested, he allowed his subconscious to go to work.

It's like when you have a great idea in the middle of

the night, and then you forget it by morning.

Note to yourself: write it down. That could be your million-dollar idea.

So when Edison fell asleep, his brain told him the other half of the equation he was missing: the charcoal principal. The charcoal principal is simply this: If you set a pile of wood on fire and then cover it with enought dirt to allow just enough of oxygen to keep the fire smoldering, but not enough to allow the wood to completely burn up, essentially this is charcoal. Edison applied that concept to the wire. He then put it into a bottle, sealed the bottle, took the air out, and BREAKTHROUGH!

The lightbulb not only did not burn up, it stayed lit for a full eight hours. This concept is still in use today. Have you ever thrown away a lightbulb or dropped a lightbulb, and it sounded like a little explosion? Well, it's because all the air is kept out so the wire burns up slowly over time. Isn't that amazing?

So persistence does pay off in the long run. Should you keep going even if you feel beat? Absolutely! Will the universe greatly assist you if it knows you're giving it your all? You better believe it! So keep going that extra mile—it may be the next thought you put into action that gives you the big payoff. And every time you turn on a light, remember Edison's story—especially when you find yourself questioning whether you should continue to pursue your dreams. And your answer will always

respectfully be, "Yes, keep going!" Thank you, Thomas Edison!

6   Spirit Cries Never

The creation of your story represents your spirit blessed with a willingness to succeed. Spirit stands for the spiritual part of a person; it's their enlightenment, their soul, their courage, and it's even their state of mind. It's our willpower. Many overachievers look to a higher source for the power of thought and ideas that radiate to them and through them. If you discover a message from your higher source—listen! If it's telling you "Don't quit," it's the universe preparing a place in history for you to explore greatness.

Your ability to recognize this and use it is entirely up to you. I've talked about brainstorming ideas. I've talked about borrowing from your future by using applied, unwavering faith. I've talked about the importance of persistence. But in the end, your level of achievement will be guided by your mind and acted upon by your flesh as a human.

The great minds of the past century have mastered the art of listening to their inner self—the one that lets them sleep well at night, the one that gives them an idea at 3:00 a.m. while they're asleep. Most people call this a hunch. I call it a defining moment—a conviction, if you will. Here

are some outstanding people you may or may not know about and the results of listening to their hunches:

Sam Walton had a hunch from his creative intelligence. Yet the masses didn't think that his ideas were worthy of exposure. Instead, he listened to his spirit cry "Never!" and as a result, Sam Walton brought big-scale retail to small towns through his company, Wal-Mart. Through sheer tenacity and pricing brilliance, Sam Walton turned Wal-Mart into the largest retailer in the world, making his shareholders and his family wealthy while changing the way consumers shop and business works.

Bill Gates had a hunch sparked by his creative intelligence. His ideas were so far-fetched that nobody wanted to listen to them. He and his partner submitted a software idea before it was even completed. He had an idea for a way to connect the world. His ability to borrow from his future is the very reason why the majority of computers in households today use a Microsoft product. His spirit cried, "Don't quit," and he listened.

Colonel Sanders' creative intelligence provided him with a hunch, too. Known today as an American fast food pioneer, he started from humble beginnings way before he developed his secret recipe. When he was forty years old, the Colonel began cooking for hungry travelers who stopped at his service station in Corbin, Kentucky. He didn't have a restaurant then, so he served folks at his

own dining room table in the living quarters attached to his service station. As more people started coming just for the food, he moved across the street to a motel with a restaurant that seated 142 people. Over the next nine years, he perfected his secret blend of eleven herbs and spices using the basic cooking technique that is still in operation today.

Walt Disney also listened to his creative intelligence. His imagination and vision led to the creation of one of the most successful entertainment businesses of all time. This came with a price, however. To support his idea, he required financial help. Walt went to 503 banks seeking a loan, and all of them refused him. On opening day of Disneyland, there were mechanical problems with the rides, so none of them were operational. How would you have felt if you were an investor who invested millions of dollars into a new venture and the first three days of the big opening drew negative publicity? Every eighteeen months for the next thirty years, Walt was on the verge of bankruptcy. His spirit crying "Never" is the reason for the Disney empire. He referred to his employees as "imaginers." Because of his willingness to listen to his spirit, we have the opportunity to enjoy the resorts and movies developed by the Disney Corporation long after his death.

Michael Jordan had a hunch that sparked his creative intelligence. Being cut from his high school varsity team was a defining moment for Michael. His spirit cried out

with a hunger for success. His coach gave him an ultimatum. He told him he wouldn't make the varsity team that year, but if Michael would practice with him every morning for one hour before school, not only would he be the most conditioned player on the team, but the next year he would make the team. And this led to him becoming a superstar.

Jordan became a MEGA star after losing to Detroit in the NBA playoffs. Back on the bus, he cried the whole way home. He promised himself that he would never be in a position like that again. His spirit not only cried "Never," it shook him up. He came back the next year and won three back-to-back championships in a row. After taking a year off to play baseball, he returned to basketball and won another three championships in a row. As a result of listening to his spirit, he has been responsible for employing more people in Chicago than ever before. He used his power for good.

As mentioned previously, Thomas Edison was definitely in tune with his infinite intelligence. People who knew him said he had a hard time paying attention, and in today's terms he probably would have been diagnosed with A.D.H.D. (Attention Deficit Hyperactivity Disorder). His spirit enabled him to use this for the good of mankind. Not only was Edison responsible for the development of the incandescent lamp, he also invented the first sound-recording machine and many, many other inventions. To be exact, Edison was awarded 1,368 separate and distinct patents during his lifetime. He passed away at age eighty-four on October 18th, 1931—the anniversary date of the invention of the incandescent lightbulb.

Jeff Bezos had a hunch that sparked his creative intelligence. Going against the odds always comes with a price. His ideas were ingenious. Using the power of the Internet, he came up with a way for consumers to buy books faster and cheaper without leaving home. The best part was that they could be delivered to wherever anyone wanted. Like any great inventor, his friends and family laughed at him and told him his idea was ridiculous. How could he even think of competing with bookstore giants like Borders or Barnes & Noble? But his spirit cried, "Never!" Within five years, Bezo's company was doing over $31 million and overall was the best place for book distribution ever. Today his company does well over a billion. Maybe you've heard of it? Amazon.com. In an interview, Bezos told everyone how his friends and family laughed at him about his little online bookstore. His final comment was, "Guess who's laughing now!"

The astronauts of Apollo 13 had an active, in-the-moment hunch—a choice between life and death that sparked the creative intelligence of many to bring them home safely from the Apollo 13 mission. With an endless amount of effort and strategy, a large group of like-minded individuals sparked a message of hope around the world. As a result, the astronauts lived to tell their story about the

power of teamwork and creative intelligence. They truly coined the phrase "Failure is not an option!" How powerful is that!

Mahatma Gandhi had a hunch that sparked his creative intelligence, and the effects expanded to a nation. Gandhi's experiences inspired him to do something that had never been done. His purpose was to end the sufferings of the people in India. At his first public speech, Gandhi called a meeting of the citizens, and he told them to form a league. It caused a new awakening among Indians. He began to teach a policy of passive resistance and noncooperation. Gandhi became the international symbol of a free India. He was beaten and then jailed for something he believed in—a cause greater than himself. His spirit cried, "Never give up," and as a result, he calmed a nation and attained victory without using a single weapon. To accomplish this, he lived a spiritual and ascetic life of prayer, fasting, and meditation. We can all learn an empowering lesson from the life of Gandhi.

So, when you get a hunch, or an idea sparked from your own creative intelligence, even if it's in the middle of the night, you'd better pay attention—you'd better recognize it. And more importantly, you'd better act upon it. Our joy and peace comes with a price; the reciprocal effect of striving and preserving could be much more than just a personal reward. The rewards could affect the world in a positive, life-changing way. When your spirit cries out to

you, telling you: "Never! Ever! Give up!"
you'd better listen.

7 HEART OF A CHAMPION

How does one become unstoppable? How does one keep getting back up after life and the world knocks them down and holds them there? Simple, but not easy. Champions carry with them the heart to do and accomplish anything. Champions are pacesetters. They go the extra mile. The champion's heart I'm describing comes in many shapes and forms.

A mother who gives unselfishly to her family and others has the heart of a champion. The man who sacrifices his dinner when he's temporarily short on food and money so his family and others can eat has the heart of a champion. An innovator who works to make this world a better place has the heart of a champion.

Ask yourself this: "Up to this point in my life, have I given it my all? Have I rendered contributions to serve others unselfishly? Do I perform random acts of kindness?" The law of attraction simply means that the way we think will become our reality by the actions we do.

Champions of the heart swallow their pride. Let me tell you, I've never heard of anyone choking and dying because they swallowed their pride! I believe that in your finest moments, you must lead your life with your heart.

Be known as a person who has heart—you will attract more respect to yourself and others. Be grateful for everything you have—and everything you don't have. Life will reward you tremendously if you do just that.

Developing the heart of a champion involves risk. It's a risk to let go of self-limiting beliefs. It's a risk to take on a more empowering identity. Your heart will be challenged if you desire to be exceptional. And only you can decide your heart's fate.

The other day my daughter and I went out for some ice cream. The man in front of us ordered ice cream for his child and himself. When it was time to pay, his credit card was declined. He opted to give the ice cream back and come back later with the money. At that point, I knew I was at the right place at the right time.

I told the cashier to stop and give that man and his child back their ice cream and I would pick up the bill. I felt such emotion come from this man, as his eyes watered up. With a soft smile and a soft voice, he said to me, "Thank you, sir."

As he was leaving, he put his head down and handed the ice cream to his child and they both walked away. You see, the more you give, the more you receive. As a result, what I received was a true moment to allow my daughter to experience the art of giving and receiving. When you give from the heart, it's a moment no one can take from you.

My daughter said, "That was awesome, Dad. I hope they enjoy their ice cream." I told her, " They will!"

So we learn many lessons by having a heart of a champion—lessons that will last a lifetime; lessons that can teach compassion and strength. Why do you think I paid for that man's ice cream? Well, there were many reasons, but one that sticks out for me is that I had seen myself doing that very thing in one of my dreams, and to bring my dream to my reality was a blessing for me. It gave me a sense of fulfillment.

What exercises can you do today that will strengthen your heart? One of the best ways is to do a random act of kindness. Call someone you've been meaning to contact. Send someone a postcard for no reason, just to thank them for being a friend, spouse, mother, father, lover, neighbor, or colleague. Watch what happens.

Your friends will become better friends. Your family relationships will be more in harmony. Imagine what this could do for your lover or spouse! Just by feeling appreciated, people will pay you back by being more of who they want to be, especially around you.

Have you ever heard anyone say, "You bring the best out in me"? It's called respect. You don't gain respect unless you lead with your heart. The heart of a champion understands this and will always go the extra mile. The heart of a champion requires constant conditioning. It

requires action! Do more. Be more. Become more. Give your heart a chance to grow, and the champion inside will come out.

Two champions of the heart are John F. Kennedy and Martin Luther King, Jr. In their famous speeches, we all learned about the ability to serve and live the life of a champion. JFK moved our nation when he told us we would be the first to reach the moon, and we were. We all remember his moving words, "My fellow Americans, ask not what your country can do for you, but what you can do for your country."

Whether you're building a family, a friendship, or a business, each situation requires that same attitude and conviction. Ask not what your family can do for you, but what you can do for your family. Ask not what your friends can do for you, but what you can do for your friends. Finally, ask not what your business colleagues can do for you, but what you can do for your business colleagues.

Martin Luther King, Jr.'s "I Have a Dream" speech makes me appreciate the freedom that a lot of people take for granted: the freedom we have to love unconditionally; the freedom we have to give unselfishly; the freedom we have to act out our most incredible dreams derived from our creative imagination; the freedom we have to pursue free enterprise. Mr. King had a dream of equality. He led with his heart, and his message was heard.

8   L<small>EADERS VS.</small> F<small>OLLOWERS</small>

Leaders leave legacies, while followers live out the ideas of leaders. Which is better: a leader or a follower? The answer is neither. They are both extremely important. When I was growing up, I heard a quote from an old movie that went like this: "Heros have great stories, but legends never die." I believe both leaders and followers are equally important. In life, business, and relationships, we require both to be effective. An extraordinary leader sets the path, while a follower follows it.

Legends are tremendous risk takers. Heroes take the same risk, but on a different level. The true reality of leaders vs. followers is that they require each other. They work in harmony to produce life-changing events.

A mother or a father could be a hero in the way they raise their children, in the life they provide for them. Many times someone describes their mother, father, or whoever raised them as the hero in their life. Some refer to a spiritual hero based on their religion. People look up to heroes and model their lives after them. Both heroes and those who admire them possess leadership qualities. Both

have strived for and developed unbreakable human spirits.

When I was first becoming an entrepreneur, I was an effective follower until I was ready to lead. I followed great leaders. I did everything they told me to do in addition to my own ability. Nobody asked me to become a leader. I just knew when the time was right.

For those of you following leaders, congratulations! It takes courage and strength to become an effective leader. And when your hunches come knocking, make sure you answer the door! Learn all you can now. Be more. Do more. Expand your vision more.

Someone asked Helen Keller if losing one's eyesight was one of the worst things that could to happen to an individual. She replied that the worst thing would be losing their vision! Modeling someone is powerful. Becoming the person you were intended to be is priceless.

Legends and heroes don't shy away from fear. They boldly step in the direction it demands of them—it's just that one steps forward first, while the other follows. The follower seeks guidance from an effective leader, while the leader seeks effective followers to stay on the path they forge. Your infinite intelligence will guide you when you are ready. When the time comes, you will take the initiative required to move forward.

Both leaders and followers play a significant part in life. We must give gratitude for all who have sacrificed.

Some have even given the ultimate sacrifice for what they believe. So here is a small tribute to some of the bravest, most innovative people that have walked the face of earth.

Try not to be a man of success, but rather to be a man of value.
- Albert Einstein

Do what you can, with what you have, where you are.
- Theodore Roosevelt

It is time for us to stand and cheer for the doer, the achiever, the one who recognizes the challenge and does something about it.
- Vince Lombardi

Many of life's failures are people who did not realize how close they were to success when they gave up.
- Thomas Edison

A leader is one who knows the way, goes the way, and shows the way.
- John C. Maxwell

*What comes out of you when you are
squeezed is what is inside you.*
- Wayne Dyer

*I've missed more than 9000 shots in my career. I've lost
almost 300 games. Twenty-six times, I've been trusted to
take the game winning shot and missed. I've failed over and
over and over again in my life. And that is why I succeed.*
- Michael Jordan

*Persistence and laser focus are the words and music of
your ultimate destiny!*
- Randy Gonzales, Jr.

My advice is to take all these quotes, type them up, and
print them out. Then find a picture of each of these leaders
and hang their quote next to their name. Do this wherever
your creative workspace is. Surround yourself with success.
It's incredible how much more productive you are when
you are surrounded with like-minded individuals. Make
them part of your Millionaire Mastermind Roundtable.

9 KNOWING WHAT IT'S LIKE

Many people want overnight success. Many people that are successful today are considered overnight successes. Being an overnight success is wonderful, but let me tell you the best way to become an overnight success. Do what you love for a long period of time, and overnight it will catch up to you! Every person that I have interviewed has had similar responses to this concept of overnight success. They all had to go through a process that allowed them to develop into who they are now. It was a learning curve. This has been true in my own life as well.

This process consists of a collaboration of our own learning combined with our own personal mentors and teachers. Some of my personal teachers and mentors are leaders like Jeffery Combs, Tony Robbins, Mark Victor Hanson, and Rev. Kenneth F. Haney. One teacher in particular who I've studied endlessly but never had the chance to meet in person is Napoleon Hill.

Every one of these mentors went through a similar process. They understand what it takes to overcome adversity. I have studied many other people, but these have

had the greatest impact on my life.

Most people never take into account that the most successful people in the world failed much more than they succeeded. Of course, their success is mentioned much more than their failures. For Thomas Edison, it was over 10,000 failures before he created the lightbulb. But that was only *one* of over 1,300 inventions. On the big scale, Thomas Edison was a huge failure. Is that why he was successful?

Michael Jordan is a mega failure as well. He has missed over 9000 shots, twenty-six of them game-winning shots. That's why people still wear his clothing to this day. He has gained respect around the world. People mirror and model themselves after Jordan because they recognize the belief in himself that he possessed, and people adopt this same belief in themselves when they are faced with adversity. It gives them inspiration for their own dreams. They understand that they only lose if they fail to keep on failing. Failing is what gets you hungry, and Michael Jordan was just that, hungry for success.

Knowing what it's like to fail before you succeed is how we grow. It's what gets us hungry for answers. I truly believe in lifelong learning. I know that the struggles we face in obtaining our goals are only part of our greatest moments coming to fruition if we allow them to.

I know what it's like to feel alone. I know what it's like to be hungry physically, mentally, spiritually, and financially.

I know what it's like to lose a friend and loved one. I know what it's like to see disappointment on the face of your child because you failed to launch your ideas with passion.

I know what it's like to be virturally homeless— embarrassed to the point that you don't want anyone to know what was going on with you. I know what it's like to not take the path of least resistance the easy way out because of my self limiting beliefs and have your soul eat at you all for a couple hundred bucks for not paying child support for the month just so I could eat. I know what it's like to have cars repossessed after missing payments three months in a row because you used your money again for food, shelter, and seeing my child on the weekends. (When I was in this situation, the rest of my money went for advertising and promoting my business, even if I didn't make a dime in return. I was willing to take the risk.)

My turning point came like that next breath of fresh air. I found mentors that taught me how to think differently. They taught me to lead with my heart and not my head. The taught me to start where I was at, even if I was afraid and didn't feel ready. I found that the best way to get moving and shaking was to start moving and shaking. I learned to track my progress, which was huge... and I'll be coming out soon with a CD to assist you with tracking your progress. Tracking my progress allowed me to look at my ratios and improve them.

I started learning how to dream big. I began to turn small dreams into large, fulfilling ones. I began to surround myself with success. I was consumed by it. I began speaking about my future in the present tense. I applied a positive mental attitude towards my definite major purpose. I learned to live my passion by giving other people a chance to grow. I experienced what it was like to cry all night, telling myself that I would never be in a position like this again, and I learned to use those emotions as fuel instead of disappointment. (Your disappointments are there to serve you, so feed off them.) Napoleon Hill said, "If you don't learn from your mistakes, you might as well not make any." Now isn't that clever! Give yourself permission to fail—learn from that experience and move foward.

I learned to accept problems with a positive mental attitude and not worry about them. I learned and applied self-discipline.

My daily actions were a result of what I wanted—not what I didn't want. I wanted to be in a position where I didn't have to do the nine-to-five grind. I wanted to be in a position to be in control of my life. I wanted to be in a position to connect with some of the great leaders of our time, instead of complaining about how lucky other people were. I found out that luck is when opportunity and preparation meet and fall in love. I got to the point where the only thing on my mind was succeeding. If something didn't serve me in a positive way—in other words, if it was not empowering—I didn't listen to it. I focused on what I could do instead of what I couldn't do.

I sought out people of influence to learn from and model. I knew success left clues, so I was constantly searching for the clues that I deserved to attract to my reality. I learned how to cooperate with others for our mutual betterment. I learned to listen to my inner voice and respect it.

Your best will come out when things are not going well, when you are at your worst. I believe this applies to everyone who has overcome adversity. Anytime I encounter adversity, I tell myself, "Come on, old self, this will make a great story someday," and I move foward. Persistance leads to action, and laser focus is the direction to any destination.

Ray Kroch knew what it was like to be laughed at by his colleagues. They mocked his ideas. Let me take you back to how things might have been the day when Ray Kroch explained his new idea to his team. It might have gone a little something like this.

> Ray: "Hey guys, I have an idea."
> Team: "Okay, Ray, let's have it."
> Ray: "I have this idea, and I have a hunch it will change the way we do business, and it will affect other restaurants as well. Number one: we will be more efficient. Number two: we will be able to serve more people, and number three: we will be able to imediately implement this

system in all of our restaurants. Here goes— instead of a traditional setting for people to dine with us, let's do away with the hostess greeting people when they come in."

Team: "You mean... no one to greet them?"

Ray: "Uh, yeah! And I have another idea."

Team: "Okay, Ray, what is it?"

Ray: "Instead of a sit-down menu, I think we should just have one menu posted on the wall for everyone to order from."

Team: "Have you lost your mind, Ray?"

Ray: "Oh yeah, and instead of being waited on by a waiter at our restaurants, why don't we have our customers wait in line to give us their order?"

Team: "Ray, for real, man, you are really on something!"

Ray: " ...and instead of having their food brought to them, why don't we have them wait for their food, and when their order is ready, they can seat themselves wherever they like. And instead of having nice cushioned seats for our customers to sit on, let's replace them with hard, uncomfortable seats so they don't stay here forever. They sit down, they eat, and they leave. And we won't require busboys anymore. Before they leave, our customers will throw their own trash away after they're done eating. This is what I want to do. Any feedback?"

Can you imagine the faces and the dropped jaws when Ray's team heard what sounded like one of the most ridiculous ways to run a future successful restaurant? But look at any chain of fast-food joints (hence the name

"fast food"). They follow this same system because it works.

This story illustrates the point that all successful entrepreneurs know what it's like to go through a process of feeling rejected for their ideas. Every successful person knows the only way to really fail is to quit on their hunches even before they get started.

So if you're flourishing, if you're working from your own inner strength, congratulations, and welcome to the process of transformation. Keep a journal, because someday soon I may be interviewing you, giving you the opportunity to inspire the world with your story of perseverance in order to fulfill your vision!

10 IT'S YOUR TURN: ACTION!

I'm extremely excited about this chapter. This is your moment to awaken the spirit within you. This is where we put everything on the line. This chapter will reveal what you're really made of. You're going to have to dig deep for this one, but the end result will be beyond your wildest dreams.

You must break out of your comfort zone. Your comfort zone is the very reason you are where you are. Together, we will increase your comfort zone, and your income zone will follow. So from this point on, there is no thinking outside the box; instead, I want you to destroy the box *in your mind*. The body cannot live without the mind, so that is the best place to start your success.

You will raise your standards from this point on, and this will become the norm. You will act like you are an admired leader. See people coming to you from around the world, seeking your message. This is where we put it all together—this is where the magic begins. The title of this chapter says it all: It's your turn! Say it out loud to yourself: "It's my turn." You must get emotional about your dreams. "It's my turn!" Say it with all your power

and might. Start believing it, and say it again. "It's MY TURN!" Close your eyes right now for thirty seconds. Say it to yourself and feel your power come from within. Fill your mind with belief, and say it. Each time you repeat this, take a deep breath, let it out slowly, and nod your head up and down to let your physiology know that it's really your turn. "IT'S MY TURN!" Do it now!

ACTION! ACTION! ACTION!

Now is your chance for greatness to catch up with all of your efforts. You will see for yourself that when your unbreakable human spirit is set free, all kinds of possibilities are within your reach. *You* set the pace. Remember, the speed of the leader is also the speed of the group. Lead by example.

Let's begin. As I always say at the end of a lecture, conference call, or training: "Live with Fulfillment, Serve with Passion, and Die with NO Regrets." This final chapter covers what it means to serve. I truly believe that you cannot live your life with fulfillment or die with no regrets if you never have served anybody with passion. Your future depends upon the service you provide.

I teach my students that investing is an important part of the Millionaire Mastermind Roundtable movement. Invest in your mind. Invest in your team. Invest in your faith. Invest in your dreams. Invest in your vision.

Investing is how we grow mentally, spiritually, physically, and financially. You can invest a little or a lot—

it's up to you. You invest for your ROI, also known as your "return on investment."

Many people are very unhappy physically and financially. My question is always, "Why?" I notice they invest their time either watching TV or taking naps. When they complain about who's doing what on certain soaps, I know why they are where they are. Are they just lazy? No—I believe they just haven't found a labor of love. As a result, they turn towards TV to fill a void in their life by watching other people live their lives.

You rarely see anybody on TV watching TV. Instead, they are always actively doing something, going somewhere, or solving some problem. What if we were to take action and accountability for our own time, money, and thoughts? Where would we be? How much further would we go? Before you know it, some people might be talking about you and your story. Your story might give them hope to take action—but only if you invest your assets wisely.

I taught my daughter a long time ago that when she was asked what she wanted from friends or family for her birthday or Christmas, she should ask for *two* of what she wanted. For example, if she wanted a new bike, I taught her to ask for two. Now she would have the ability to rent one bike out for revenue and enjoy the other for pleasure.

She understood the concept so well that when I was showing her some of my real estate investment deals, she asked me how could she get involved with me in real estate

as a partnership! Today she is following my lead, but someday she might be the leader. My daughter is acquiring knowledge, and she is learning to put it into action—all before her thirteenth birthday!

Successful networkers put this principle into practice. That means whether you haven't made a dime this month or you earned $100,000, it doesn't matter to your subconscious. So don't just buy one of these books, invest in three to five of them. If you are a person seeking enlightenment, keep one for yourself, give one to someone you love (remember to fill out the dedication page!), and give one to someone you don't trust. Wow! For most of you, at first this may seem tough, but remember that you want to be at peace with yourself and hold no grudges when you are pursuing greatness. This shows the universe your willingness to be a person who seeks good for all mankind. More doors will open up for you, because you will be more open to receive.

Let's say you can't think of someone you don't trust. How about giving one to a neighbor you haven't met? How about an ex-spouse or lover? Let's say your child has a teacher they don't like very much. Give a copy of this book to your child, have your child sign the dedication page for this teacher, and watch what happens!

Sometimes our enemies can be very valuable. Find out why they don't like you. Listen to what they say about you, and then do a quick evaluation to see if what they say

is true. If it's not, don't pay any attention to them. The point is to always go into every situation with a positive, active, open mind.

If you are building a team, invest in one book for yourself, another for someone you love, and three more for your Millionaire Mastermind Roundtable. Who do you allow into your Millionaire Mastermind Roundtable? Let me give you a checklist. If someone only has two of the three characteristics, do not let them into your MMR group. They can do more damage than anything. They *MUST* posses all three qualities. Here they are:

> 1. *Loyalty—They must be loyal.*
> 2. *Dependability—They must be dependable.*
> 3. *Ability—They must posses the ability to take action.*
> *(If their skills are not up to par, are they willing to learn and proceed exactly as you ask them? No exceptions!)*

This is how you determine whom to include in your Millionaire Mastermind Roundtable.

Lifelong learning is how we renew our faith and how we grow. It's the cleansing of our minds from the inside out. It gives us clarity mentally, physically, spiritually, and financially.

It's the same reason we take showers every day. We want to cleanse our bodies of any residual physical dirt. And every day we gather some sort of mental dirt, or even financial dirt. The seven-million-dollar question is: "How

do we sustain a healthy mental attitude?" It's simple. It's through the books we read and the CDs we constantly listen to.

Why do you clean your home and surroundings? Because it builds your self-worth. That's why you just don't invest in one book for yourself—you invest in three to five books. If you lived with someone that *never, ever* took showers or cleaned up after themselves, after a while it would drive you absolutely insane. But if you shared with them the importance of cleanliness or picking up after themselves, you would at least have given them the opportunity to understand your views, and it might motivate them to take action.

When you're building a team, a lot of your team members may not have a positive mental attitude—that's the main reason they struggle and quit. Their vision is clouded by negativity. Your goal is to create instantaneous behavioral change by giving them an alternative way of thinking and living. They just might wake up one day and model themselves after you. (And if you think, "I hope they don't model after *me*," you'd better read this book more than once. You'd better listen to your CDs more than once.)

Here are my steps for developing the mental and spiritual clarity that will allow yourself and those around you to flourish. This is a list of requirements for achieving seven-figure RESULTS. If you follow these steps, by this

simple act of discipline you will have fulfilled the initial serving portion of your success. As a result, you will have no regrets, and without a shadow of a doubt, you will blossom into living a life of fulfillment. Here is your simple checklist:

1. **Invest in three to five copies of *The Unbreakable Human Spirit.*** *My studies have shown that there is greater retention and momentum when teams work in unison for a greater cause. For enlightenment, pick up three books: one for you, one for a loved one, and one for someone you want to empower (a neighbor, an enemy, or someone you don't know well that shows resistance to you). Using my simple checklist with action and enthusiasm will cause your income and your network to skyrocket.*

2. **Fill out the Dedication Page.** *Have someone take a picture of you dedicating the book to the recipient of your choice, mail it with one of our proven cards, and then watch your business and someone you care about blossom. It's a beautiful thing!*

3. **Invest in the two-part CD series, *Within My Reach – How to Play.*** *If you're growing a networking or direct sales business, this next step is a MUST! Part 1 consists of eight CDs featuring millionaires sharing some of the top secrets in our industry. You'll learn what to say, how to say it, and when to say it. Eveyone that I've placed on this system has doubled their income in forty-five days. Results may vary, but this has been my personal experience with my clients. Part 2: Within My Reach - Practical*

> *Actions of a Millionaire will greatly assist you in creating a massive impact. You see, I deserve to have you become another six- or seven-figure testimonial. We have one of the greatest opportunities to go out and create a difference one partner at a time.*

As soon as you have completed these simple steps, you will then find your first three people to invite to your Millionaire Mastermind Roundtable. These are people who have followed these same simple steps as well. Send me a letter via snail mail to:

Millionaire Mastermind Roundtable
P.O. Box 497
Fair Oaks, CA 95628

I will send you an *Official Millionaire Mastermind Roundtable Certificate.*

Take one step up, and then inspire and lead your team to do the same. Learn to give them a hand up instead of a handout. You're an inspiration; welcome to a world of possibility!

Your colleague, coach, and friend,

Randy Gonzales, Jr

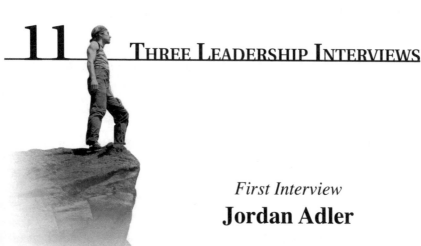

First Interview
Jordan Adler

Today we have the privilege of hearing from Jordan Adler on the subject of developing your human spirit. Jordan resides in the small ghost town of Jerome, Arizona, where he lives in his dream home overlooking Verde Valley in Sedona, Arizona. Jordan reminds me of the famous quote, "People won't remember what you say or do, but they will remember how you made them feel." I met Jordan in 1999, and we have remained friends and colleagues through almost a decade of teaching wealth to others. Jordan has developed many such relationships throughout the years and throughout the world. So enjoy this interview with my good friend and colleague, Mr. Jordan Adler. Thank you, Jordan, for taking some time to speak with me today.

JORDAN: It's my pleasure.

RANDY: So Jordan, where did you grow up?

JORDAN: I grew up in south suburbs of Chicago, Illinois.

RANDY: Tell me a little bit about your family. Did you have any major influences growing up?

JORDAN: No, actually my father was a working-class guy; he had

a series of jobs throughout my childhood. I grew up in a family of five—myself, two sisters, and my parents lived in a little home in the south suburbs of Chicago. I really did not know any entrepreneurs growing up. Everyone in our neighborhood was employed by a company, and the average income in my neighborhood was $25,000 - $35,000 a year.

RANDY: When did you decide to be an entrepreneur?

JORDAN: Even when I was very young, I had entrepreneurial characteristics and qualities. I liked to build things, I liked to like to create things—I was always building things from raw materials around our house. I would invent things out of toilet paper rolls and scotch tape... I'd just create these contraptions, and then I would put on puppet shows and charge people a quarter to come to them. I used to have a lemonade stand, and I delivered papers—all that stuff that kids do to make a little extra money. I had entrepreneurial qualities, but I didn't know what that was back then.

RANDY: What major challenges and problems did you face, and how did you handle them in the beginning?

JORDAN: Well, I was the guy that would always get picked last for the sports teams in elementary and high school. I was fairly short and a little bit overweight, and nobody wanted me on their team. They didn't want me on the basketball team, they didn't want me on the soccer team, and they didn't want me on their football team. I can remember being pissed off that nobody picked me. Looking back, it's kind of ironic, because today, what do I do? I create teams! I'm the number one team builder in our company—I let everybody on my team.

RANDY: Wow, that is a unique was of looking at it. So what major challenges or problems did you face as an adult?

JORDAN: You know, you're always faced with challenges; challenges are just part of life. It's really how you look at those challenges and what they mean to you that ultimately will determine your outcome. I can think of a few specific examples in my network marketing career. Most of of us who get involved in network marketing think it's going to be our ticket out of corporate America, our ticket to freedom and residual income. We want the freedom to live the life we always dreamed of.

I can remember being a brand-new rep in my company. I was making less than $1500 a month, and I had an opportunity to go to Massachusetts and show the business to a group of people there. I had a team with about thirty people. I remember flying there on borrowed money; I took a little cash advance on my credit card because I really didn't have the money. I was upside down financially—my bills exceeded my income. But I took a risk and flew there, rented a car, and drove in a snowstorm. The drive took me about two-and-a-half hours, instead of the twenty minutes it would have normally taken. I was in my early thirties, and I showed up at this house, and nobody from my team showed up. Not one person showed up, not even the person running the meeting, and all the lights were out in the house. So there I was, standing on the doorstep in this blizzard after traveling a couple thousand miles to go to this meeting on borrowed money, money that I didn't have. I had a decison to make; I had a choice to make standing there on that doorstep. Do I quit at this point, like all the other things that I'd been involved in? Or do I decide that if anybody is going to be successful at this, it's me?

That was a major turning point for me. I decided to stay with it. My whole group quit. What happened was that there were a couple of glitches with our system, and the group got negative and they all decided that it wasn't worth it. The snowstorm was just another reason not to show up, and nobody called me to let me know that they weren't going to be there. That was a major turning point for me in my network marketing career, because I had been in several other network marketing companies prior to this one, and I had quit all of them. At that moment I decided that I wasn't going to quit this one. I decided I was going to see the job through—I chose to stick with it and work through those challenges, and ultimately I went on to build a team of tens of thousands of people. I made millions of dollars with that company, but it took me three to four years before I started earning any money worth talking about.

RANDY: Wow! That's a very inspiring story. You stuck with it and you stood your ground— that's the unbreakable human spirit. Many people took the easier route, whereas you took the road less traveled. We've been friends and colleagues for many years, and I've personally seen you motivate and inspire others to tap into their own unbreakable human spirit. What motivates you?

JORDAN: You know, I think motivation is a by-product of having hope, of having something to look forward to. If you have a great vacation planned, you're usually pretty motivated because you're really looking forward to that vacation—especially if it's a vacation you really want to take. You have something positive to look forward to. People who don't have anything to look forward to in life typically are pretty depressed. When you lose hope, you get depressed. So in the world of entrepreneurs, you are responsible for creating what it is you have to look forward to. You create your

future by what you put into your schedule.

Here's an example. Somebody could say, "I have never really taken a great vacation." They could go through their whole life being depressed and feeling deprived, when in reality they could take their pen and write that vacation on their calendar, and then plan for it and have something great to look forward to. That's creating your future.

The reason most people get involved in a business opportunity is that there's something really compelling to look forward to. They glimpse a bright future, a future filled with freedom, travel, and fulfilled dreams. That opportunity is going to provide them with unlimited residual income, new friends, and travel, etc. But what happens? They go out and get three or four people, those people end up becoming negative, and so they feel stupid for getting involved in an opportunity. All that hope gets minimized. What happens to their motivation? They start to get depressed, right? What they had to look forward to has been suddenly taken away from them, so they're not as hopeful. I think the key to motivation is to keep your outcome in front of you and to create opportunities for yourself, because that's your responsibility as an entrepreneur. No one else is going to do it for you; you create those opportunities to grow, to learn, and to keep yourself inspired.

RANDY: Chapter Two of my book talks about the importance of borrowing from your future by utilizing applied faith. In your journey, have you ever had to stop for a moment, dig deep, and look at what could be instead of what would be? If so, how did you go about doing it?

JORDAN: Absolutely. After being with my company for thirteen years, there was a shift in the market that caused one of

our key products to be obsolete. As a result, that opportunity which had been a really rich opportunity for many years disappeared. I had a huge five-figure monthly income, and my overhead was $20,000 a month. When that company folded, my cash flow disappeared, and I found myself starting over. Even though I had plenty of savings and some real estate investments, my monthly expenditure was $20,000 a month, so without cash flow I went through $20,000 a month in four months. I refinanced my home; I went through $80,000 in cash in four months. My future was uncertain; I didn't know what I was going to do next. Well, I aligned myself with another company. In this company, the biggest check they paid out up to that point was $3,000-$4,000 a month—and I needed $20,000 a month just to break even. However, I chose to get involved because I saw the opportunity. I stepped out a hundred percent on faith, knowing: A) the money was there and B) I could get it. All the experts in the industry that I talked to said, "Great idea, great service, but you'll never make any money." And you know what? I didn't listen to them, because my intuition (my gut) told me that there was something really substantial there when I imagined millions of people using this service. So I went for it, and I'm sure glad I did, because that leap of faith led me to an income that far exceeded what I had ever made in my life.

RANDY: Wow, that's some tremendous intestinal fortitude! As a leader, and even more importantly, as a human being, how does one develop intestinal fortitude and persistence?

JORDAN: You can't make decisions based on emotion. If you're making decisions based on how you feel on any given day, you'll never do what you need to do to get the job done. There will be many days when you won't feel like going out and getting to work.

However, if you make your decision based on your commitment, then you work whether you're having a good day or a bad day. The reality is we all have good days and we all have really bad days. If you base your decisions on this, then you're not going to do much work on your bad days. Instead say, "What am I up to in life? What's my ultimate mission? What's my goal, what am I about?" Focus on those things and work on those things regardless of how you feel on any given day.

RANDY: What is the most difficult decision to make in one's personal development?

JORDAN: A big part of it is getting out of your own way. There's so much inner conversation that keeps us from doing what we are really about. Many of the conversations we have are destructive—the conversation that says, "I'm not sure if I'm up for this challenge; I'm not smart enough; I don't know if I have the stamina; maybe it's too late; maybe I don't have the skills; maybe I'm not well prepared..." All these little conversations we have with ourselves keep us from moving toward our dreams and our goals. Getting out of our own way quiets those conversations; it's really keeping your focus on your main goal and not focusing on those conversations, because they're all made up, and they're keeping you from doing what it is you're really about.

I think charisma or having a charismatic nature is a very illusive thing; it's really difficult to define. There are a lot of ways to describe charisma, but to create charisma requires finding your passion—being true to what you really believe in and going after it with enthusiasm. When you do that, people see charisma in you. It's an energy. When someone walks into the room and you notice that person....

RANDY: ...you feel that vibration!

JORDAN: Yeah, you feel that energy with that person. It doesn't matter how tall you are, how short they are, whether they are fat or skinny, when you see that person, you just know that they're up to some big things, and you know they're going to make a difference; you feel it in their presence, because they're being true to themselves. When you're true to yourself, you're not trying to be something you're not. When you're really being true to yourself, it comes through as charisma. That energy flows out of you to other people.

RANDY: And it goes along with the law of attraction, too—whether you're attracting the right type of people or not. Do you believe that balance is important mentally?

JORDAN: I happen to have a unique perspective on balance. I think balance can be a little destructive, because as soon as you achieve balance, essentially you become stifled. It's like if you were to put you finger in a glass of water and then pull it out, what happens to that hole where your finger was? It fills up with water, right? Well, an imbalance was created when you pulled your finger out of the water. That's where growth comes from. If you think about how plants grow, it's like Anthony Robbins said, "Things grow with uncertainty." Uncertainty is a place of imbalance, but that's the only place growth happens—with uncertainty. As soon as everything becomes certain, it might feel comfortable—but there's no growth. So I don't know if the goal is to find balance. Balance is comfortable, it's nice, but if you want to grow and learn and expand, then you'll want to put yourself in a place of imbalance.

RANDY: That's awesome, Jordan. Thank you so much for your sincerity and time. Can I expect to hear from you again in my sequel, *The Unbreakable Human Spirit for Network Marketers*?

JORDAN: If you ask me to be in it, I'll be in it.

RANDY: Then let's consider it done!

Second Interview
Scott and Molly Aguilar

Listen up, all you young entrepreneurs. Scott and Molly are some of the youngest, most inspirational entrepreneurs I've seen over the past decade. Their young spirits have filled many lives with joy and prosperity. They lead by example and have a crystal clear vision of what they are seeking as well as what they deserve. They know what they're talking about, since they have been students of the game for over a decade, and they still take the initiative to learn more. It is my sincere privilege to interview Scott and Molly Aguilar.

RANDY: So let's hear a little bit about your story. Where did you guys grow up?

MOLLY: We both grew up in Arnold, CA near the Sierra Nevada mountains.

RANDY: I know exactly where that is. As a young kid, I used to go camping up there!

MOLLY: Yeah! I personally lived there for nineteen years.

RANDY: How about you, Scott?

SCOTT: Yep, I grew up in the same area. I was born in San Jose, CA, but when I was in the fifth grade, my family moved to the Sierra Nevada area. Funny story—they lost all my grades in the move, so I got to start all over in a new school, and I was no longer a D or an F student. They thought I was an A student, which was

very funny. As a result of that, I think I was treated a little differently.

RANDY: Wow, that is actually kind of funny. Tell me about your family life. Did you have any major influences growing up?

SCOTT: For myself, my major influence was my dad—in terms of business and mindset and out-of-the-box thinking, entrepreneurial thinking. He's always been an entrepreneur. He owned his own construction company, as well as his own consulting company for many years. From being in constuction, and then more recently in the consulting field, he was actually involved in a few network marketing companies when I was younger. I got turned on to reading books and listening to tapes at a very young age, and I just got the idea of all that's possible. My dad is the type of guy that could say anything to anybody. You'd get him on a jet, and he would say, "I'm buying that jet in the near future!" So we had the opportunity to go on jets and drive in Ferraris, because he told the salespeople that he would be buying one soon. He was always thinking out of the box, which had a huge impact on me.

RANDY: And that has had a major impact on your decisions today, correct?

SCOTT: Absolutely.

RANDY: OK, Molly, how about you—were there any major family influences in your life growing up?

MOLLY: Randy, It was almost the opposite for me in terms of a huge family influence. I was raised in a really traditional background with some great parents, and I didn't have the opportunity to do anything or be anything or think out of the box. I didn't have any major influences until I was nineteen, when I actually started in the business world. That's when I really grabbed on to certain people telling me to believe in myself, to believe in what was possible. I began to believe that you really could make it huge and do something in your life in a big, big kind of way.

RANDY: This question is for both of you. When did you guys decide to become entrepreneurs?

SCOTT: I decided to become an entrepreneur at the age of eighteen. My first network marketing venture was a phone company. My dad brought me into that company as a rep, and initially I didn't take it too seriously. I didn't do anything for a year, but then I went back home and really started building my business. After stepping briefly into the world of the j-o-b, I had a quick awakening to the fact that it's not very cool working for someone else; it didn't fire me up at all.

MOLLY: Basically it was the same for me. I became an entrepreneur at age nineteen. At that point, I didn't even know what the word "entrepreneur" meant, but I found out, and now I'm twenty-eight years old. I've been an entrepreneur all this time, and I will never go back.

RANDY: In your journey, what major problems and challenges did you face, and how did you handle them?

MOLLY: One of the major things I've faced was to emotionally be able to handle challenges—to go through ups and downs and still

stay focused on what it was I wanted. I learned that doing anything huge in life—becoming wealthy, creating a fortune for yourself, whatever business you're in—means it's not all going be roses along the way. So for me, it was the emotional aspect was usually the challenge.

To keep myself at a point where my commitment was larger than my emotions was really big for me. Keeping myself focused on my commitment was my major goal at that time... keeping my goals in place and not letting my feelings on that particular day or week have so much of an effect on my outcome. It was an emotional challenge learning to be strong in business, experiencing nos and rejection, going through business cycles... just learning how to handle all of that.

RANDY: It's amazing what you will discover on the journey. I've seen you guys personally motivate and inspire a tremendous amount of people to actually tap into their own unbreakable human spirit. What motivates you?

SCOTT: My own internal motivation comes from "the big man upstairs." Another thing that motivates me is just not quitting. My dad was involved in many different things, and he also quit many different things. He never stuck with one thing long enough—it was like a magnifying glass moving all over the place, trying to heat up every little thing, trying to burn anything and everything. One thing that motivates me is winning in a huge way and helping other people win. We do a lot of just leading by example.

MOLLY: For me, Randy, I'm here looking at my dream boards in my office, and I see a lot of things that motivate me. I see them on a daily basis, and it's really awesome to be focused on something,

to have a goal, and then have it become a reality. Every time that has happened to us, whether it's something simple or whether it's the car we drive, or the home we own, or the wedding we had, we created it. Knowing all that we created and turned into our reality—knowing that I can do this, that motivates me. Also believing in other people and watching them begin to succeed motivates me, because I know when I was building my business back in the early, early days, other people's beliefs that I could succeed really got me to believe in myself and gave me motivation until I found my own.

RANDY: That brings me to my next topic. Chapter Two of my book talks about the importance of borrowing from your future by utilizing applied, unwavering faith—that's the faith of action. Have you guys ever had to stop for a moment and dig down deep and look at *what could be* instead of *what's currently*? If so, how did you go about doing it?

SCOTT: People borrow from their current and past emotions; they're going to borrow from somewhere, so they might as well borrow from the future. We've been able to create a big enough picture of where we're going to be able to borrow emotion from that point. Who cares about where you're at right now? Emotionally, you don't have to be there. We've been doing this for years—especially in the beginning of our business when we didn't have anything to show for maybe three or four years. When we were just getting our business going, maybe we didn't have anything to show for it—but *emotionally* we didn't live in an 800 sq. ft. apartment; *emotionally* we didn't drive a Honda Civic. Emotionally we weren't there. Even now, I'm standing here in this beautiful house, I'm not even here, man. Right now, emotionally I'm in Fiji. I'm putting up a resort on

a private island, I just got back from spearfishing, and the sunburn on my back is a little heated—I'm going to go sit under a palm tree and sip out of a coconut for a while.

RANDY: That's outstanding! I can actually see you doing that. I like to call it "borrowing from your dreams!"

MOLLY: I'm going be there, too—that sounds awesome. The concept of borrowing from the future has been one of the most important things to me in terms of going through a hard time or a down time. I've also learned to be happy with what I have and where I am at the same time. One of my favorite quotes is "You have to enjoy what you have while pursuing what you want." Otherwise you're never happy with what you have. I remind myself daily to be really grateful and thankful for everything, but to still borrow from the future.

SCOTT: Another vision I have to share with you: I'm going to be so excited to sit at a dinner table in Turkey with fifteen key leaders from every part of the world. It's a leadership dinner, and everyone is speaking a different language.

RANDY: It's incredible to have such a crystal-clear vision, Scott. Now as a leader, and more importantly as a human being, how does one develop this type of intestinal fortitude and persistence that you're talking about?

MOLLY: It's deciding that they can do it. Everyone can, but they have to make the choice that they're going to make it and be willing to put up with circumstances along the way. It's being focused and dedicated to what you want—deciding that you can do it and not

be influenced by outside forces but by internally influencing yourself and developing yourself.

RANDY: I call it taking a hundred percent responsibility for your life.

SCOTT: Often what happens is that people sabotage themselves—I see it all the time. People focus on multiple streams of income, and that's great. But first, be focused on making your first million, and then you can go for the multiple streams. It's important to be totally focused on one thing until you get that one thing down. But what happens most of the time is that people dilute their effectiveness and start entertaining other thoughts. They start entertaining other ideas and concepts, and without knowing it, they're diluting the vibration of what they intend to make happen. So they're just destroying their own personal momentum by entertaining these thoughts. It may not seem like a big deal at the time, but their energy and their vibration is not as pure asif they were a hundred percent focused on what they're doing.

RANDY: Scott, what is the most important decision someone can make in terms of personal development?

SCOTT: The most important decision a person can make about personal development is to choose where you want to go and then go there. Making a choice and being completely focused until you get to the end result you created from day one and not veering off to some different angle is key.

RANDY: What was one of your greatest moments, and what has it meant to you as far as achievement goes?

SCOTT: Probably one of the greatest moments for me was when we got into the top performance council. Out of a million people, we attained the top fifty money-earner position in a multibillion-dollar company. To this day I still proudly wear my ring, because to me it's like a Super Bowl ring. It was huge to finally be where the top people are and be able to be looked at and spoken to with a different level of respect.

MOLLY: For me, it was the same moment. That was the proudest day of my entire life. I remember while we were driving, we received a phone call from corporate saying we had made it. I remember I started crying. I was so excited; I couldn't believe it. I just kept crying and crying out of joy. I think what it meant to me was that all our work over the years had paid off. My respect level for myself meant at that moment that I knew I could actually do it. It opened my mind to what else I could accomplish. I knew at that moment that I could do whatever I wanted to do if I put my mind to it and worked hard.

RANDY: I remember that like it was yesterday. I was there with you guys, and I was so proud of you. You inspired me with your accomplishment. I want to thank you personally for not giving up! Moments like these inspire me. It's people that go through adversity. They go through hard times. They go through good times. Most people only see what people have accomplished—rarely do they see someone's journey from start to finish.

When you guys prepare to build for the future, what thoughts go through your minds?

SCOTT: It's what thoughts we *don't* let go through our minds. I'm

talking about the law of vibrations. It's coming from a state of knowing what you're doing, of making it happen. Whatever you move toward moves toward you. You'd be surprised who wants to follow a leader who knows where they're going. It's amazing.

RANDY: A lot of my readers are business builders. So whether someone is building an organization or raising a family, can you give some examples of teamwork that you use to stay connected with the people that surround you?

MOLLY: It's important to support your significant other in their strengths as well as their weaknesses. For example, some of Scott's strengths are my weaknesses and visa versa. We seek to bring out the best in each other. To make our relationship successful, we don't criticize each other.

SCOTT: On that same note, as a couple we learned early on that if both people in a car want to hold the steering wheel, one of two things will happen. You're either going to crash and burn, or you're going to figure out that you both need to be in your own car. So that's what we did. When Molly stepped up, she didn't use the excuse that she was a young woman. She didn't entertain any of that type of stuff. She just went out there and started making it happen. I was making it happen on my end, so we had two totally different separate teams. Even though our teams are in the same organization, a lot of them don't even know each other!

MOLLY: I remember the day I decided to take control. I used to just support Scott; I didn't do the business to the extent that he did. I would show up at his presentations to help out. One day, I was at one of Scott's presentations, and as I was sitting there listening to him, I told myself, "I can do better than this." And that was the day I decided to take the brakes off and begin doing my own presentations. I started building my own team. The decision to do that, followed by his encouragement was awesome.

RANDY: As a couple, this seems like a true blessing—working in harmony with one another, allowing each other to grow at your own pace. That's incredible. What other blessings have you gained through this process?

MOLLY: Being able to grow together versus growing apart allows us to relate to each other. Putting a hundred percent effort into the same thing keeps us growing together.

RANDY: I believe this is how successful couples grow spiritually, mentally, and financially. Being able to recognize each other's strengths and weaknesses and be able to turn those weakness into strengths is very powerful indeed.

About three years ago I started a movement to raise our standards. People in my organization are operating at the highest levels, and they expect their mastermind groups to do the same. I coined a phrase called the Millionaire Mastermind Roundtable. I would love you to be part of my movement of teaching abundance and wealth to the world.

SCOTT & MOLLY: We would love to!

RANDY: One last thing... for everyone who is building a business, how important is it to track your progress?

MOLLY: Randy, It is extremely important. I'm glancing at my calendar all the time. I asked one of my reps recently what her goals for the week were. She replied, "I don't know." I told her, "Well, now it's time to define some!" By tracking your progress, you can look back and determine what was good, what was bad, and what could improve. You can discover where your weaknesses are. This allows you to reflect, and ultimately you become better. This is what helped me become better, and I recommend it to any one seeking success. Ask your team to follow this same method. You can tell them when you notice something that's throwing them off track. It holds everybody, including yourself, accountable.

SCOTT: Free enterprise is all about results. By tracking your progress, if something produces a result, then do it.

RANDY: Scott and Molly, thank you so much for your time and sincerity. You have given our readers a lot of outstanding material to grow their human spirit. Can we hear from you again in my sequel *The Unbreakable Human Spirit for Network Marketers*, which will be a more detailed look at the principles of successful business building?

SCOTT & MOLLY: Absolutely!

Third Interview
Steve Little

It's time for me to introduce to you an extraordinary man who knows how to lead from his heart, not his head. Going through the process of success has led Steve Little to teach wealth through enlightenment. He emphasizes the value of serving and has been rewarded far beyond his expectations. I connected with Steve and was instantly drawn to his vision and his execution of enlightened abundance practices. From an early age, success was imbedded into him through a series of events. As you will see, Steve is a servant to us all. It is an honor to introduce you to Mr. Steve Little.

RANDY: Steve, where did you grow up?

STEVE: Well, I moved around a bit. I was born is Syracuse, New York. However, my dad was involved in the Apollo space program, so we moved to Florida, and I spent a lot of years in the Daytona/ Cape Canaveral area. Then my dad started working in the defense department, and so most of my teenage formative years were spent in the Washinton, D.C. area. I went to college in Richmond, Virginia. So I've always lived in the eastern central U.S.

RANDY: Steve, tell me a little bit about your family. Did you have any major influences growing up?

STEVE: Early on in my life, around the age of five, I made a decision that in order to get ahead I would work really hard. Looking back, good or bad, that was the decision I made. I think that was influenced by observing my dad, who was a very typical baby boomer. He

107

worked long hours. He was committed to his job. He was definitely following the work ethic formula taught in school. So I modeled that. I would probably say that was my greatest influence was my father.

RANDY: So when did you decide to become an entrepreneur?

STEVE: (laughing) It was around age seven, when I decided the way a person creates value and worth is by producing a lot—which we know now is not necessarily the case. Back then, at age seven or eight, I started a garage cleaning service. I would tell my neighbors that I would clean their garage for them on a Saturday, something most men hated to do anyway. So I go paid a few bucks for coming in and cleaning out the garage. For me it was a really cool business, because I would find all this stuff they didn't want. I was like a pack rat. I would gather everybody's junk and bring it to my house.

I would also charge my dad a lot more than I would charge anybody else. That was the entrepreneurial thread that started at a very young age. By the time I was thirteen, I had a very substantial lawn care business. I wasn't just cutting a few yards; I was managing everyone's property in my neighborhood. That's how I created my perception of value, and that has continued throughout my career. The first two years in college I carried a heavy load—about twenty-one credit hours per semester. I didn't really go to college to enjoy college. I went to college to get finished with college.

The framework I have operated on my whole life was, "Finish, I have to finish." "I have to work hard so I can be finished." That's the way I approached college, but I quit college after two years because I realized that finishing didn't matter. I wanted to get into the world and produce. I didn't produce anything in college, I was just learning. Now it was time for me to go produce.

108

So I dropped out of school and started a cabinetmaking business, which leveraged a passion I had developed in high school around my woodworking shop. Eventually I employed about fifteen cabinetmakers. We started to do large-scale commercial fixture work. We did restaurants and banks, and I had a contract to do all the ABC stores in Virginia. This exposed me to a number of construction companies, large-scale general contracting firms— one of which ultimately acquired me and put me in charge of his construction operations. I went from cabinetmaker to commercial fixture maker to general contractor almost by default.

RANDY: That alone is amazing, Steve.

STEVE: For about six years, I had a very successful business. I had a large team of carpenters, cabinetmakers, roofers, and painters. I operated that business out of my pickup truck. I was having a lot of fun, but I had a bigger vision. One day, as I was driving to my warehouse in Richmond, Virginia, I was looking up at a new skyscraper that was going up, and the big sign at the top said "Omni Construction." My vision was that I wanted to be the next Omni Construction. I set off on that path, believing that I would achieve it by working harder and harder.

One day I had lunch with an individual who was employed at the executive level at Omni Construction. We were discussing a subcontract to do a lot of the bathroom fixture work. I was twenty-years-old at the time. He asked me what my dreams and aspirations were, and I told him I wanted to be the next Omni. He said, "Wow, that's really, really big—you do know that Omni is one of the largest national organizations in the world?" I said, "So what? There is no reason why I can't do it. I had the largest lawn care business in my neighborhood by age twelve." We had a nice conversation, and he

109

said, "Look, I don't want to discourage you—you're a wonderful guy and clearly you are on a mission to do great things, but I want you to know that if there ever was a Mr. Omni, he never hammered a nail in his life. He didn't get there the way you are going. I'm not saying it's impossible. I'm just saying it hasn't been done the way you are doing it."

It didn't discourage me, but I started to do some serious investigation into what it really take to get big projects and be the biggest company. What I realized was that Omni had a staff of people to do all kinds of things I had no knowledge of. So, at that juncture I decided to scale back my company, go back to school, get my degree, and learn how to build a real business. And it was a series of fortunate events that caused me to seek out the teaching, the training, the mentoring, and the relationships that would take me to the next level. The lesson I learned was that life is all about relationships.

RANDY: Relationships, in my experience, always make the pie so much sweeter!

STEVE: For me, this was all an experiment. When I look back, I find it amazing. There is truth to the statement, "When the student is ready, the teacher will appear." With every phase, I became ready for something else, and the teacher, the mentor, the coach, the lunch with the executive, or whomever it was, appeared. I can recount that story over and over again with an infinite number of instances.

For instance, there is a gentleman by the name of Charles E. Smith who is one of the wealthiest land developers in the Washington D.C. area. I had a contract and I was working on fixtures in his office complex. Have you ever heard of Crystal City?

RANDY: Not off the top of my head...

STEVE: Crystal City is an amazing place; it's just outside of Washington D.C., across the river. It's an office complex on the surface, but underground there is an amazing shopping mall. What was really amazing about this project is that Mr. Smith won the land in a poker game. Originally it was a railroad stockyard, and he developed it into one of the nicest office/residential complexes in the area. And he obviously became very wealthy. I was working in his office building one day, and I just thought he was just some older gentleman sitting in the office. He didn't have a "I'm the big guy" aura about him.

So we started talking. I went and got my lunch cooler, and we started having lunch and talking. He asked me what my aspirations where. I told him I wanted to be independent and financially secure so I could play with my family whenever I wanted. He nodded and said that was good, but that everyone wants that. I said, "Yeah, but I'm going to get it." He asked me an interesting question... he said, "Randy, where did you park today?" I thought that was an odd question. He said, "When you came to work today, where did you park your car?" I told him I had parked in the parking lot downstairs that was attached to the building. He said, "What do you pay for parking there?" I said, "A few bucks." He said, "It's six bucks a day to park there—did you know that?" I said, "No, but what are you getting at?" And he replied, "Do you realize that three blocks away there is a parking lot that only costs two and a half bucks a day? Do you understand the difference?" I said, "Mathematically, you mean?" He said, "No, you just wasted three and a half bucks." I thought to myself, *What are you talking about, old man?*

At that juncture, he introduced himself to me. He said, "I'm Charles E. Smith." At that point I was like, "Omigosh, I'm sitting in the big guy's office, and the big guy is here!" And he went on to say, "Steve,

111

you have great aspirations, but I've got to tell you, if you don't start parking in the two and a half dollar parking lot when it is available…you will never reach your goal." Now that was his opinion, but I can tell you this… that planted a seed in my mind. From then on, I started looking at things differently. Now, I have to admit, I didn't become a miser. I probably waste more than I should. But I do at least stop and think about it. Do I really need to valet my car? Why don't I just park in a lot and walk up the street? In fact, there have been many books written about this topic: how do the wealthy become wealthy? They don't waste what they have, among other things.

RANDY: That is an awesome story. In Chapter Two of my book, I talk about the importance of borrowing from your future by utilizing applied faith. In your journey, did you ever have to stop for a moment to dig deep and look at what could be versus what was happening at the time? How did you go about doing it?

STEVE: I do it constantly—more so now than ever, because now there is a level of an awareness that I never had. But clearly, in many of the transitions I just outlined, in every instance you really have to stop and say, "Where is this taking me? What do I need to do?" I think in the context of that point in my life, everything was defined by "What do I need to do? What do I need to get? What do I need to have?" It wasn't until later in life when I started to appreciate and to focus on "Who is it I need to be?" Unfortunately, that's the way it is for most of us; we don't recognize this until we are a little more mature.

RANDY: Steve, why do you think most people fail to start over after being faced with opposition? Most people set a goal and set out

with a dream. They have ambitions and drive, and
then when they are faced with the first opposition (such as receiving
a "no" or being told their idea is dumb), they tend to listen to the
people who are not going to help them reach their goal anyway. In
your option, why is that?

STEVE: I think people develop a belief system on what is and
isn't possible in their lives. Goals and aspirations are set outside of
that belief system. Now, the belief system is oftentimes a limiting
belief system. So when people encounter opposition, it affirms their
limiting beliefs, or it confirms that they can't do what they thought
they already couldn't do. It is just confirmation that they are limited
to whatever the limiting belief is. So they go back to that.

We've seen this in particular in the network marketing world. You
run into someone who has disengaged and they say, "You know what,
I just couldn't do it. I just couldn't succeed in network marketing."
In terms of opportunity, I can't think of any other industry that
will give more people more opportunity to succeed than network
marketing. Anyone can do networking marketing, IF THEY ARE
WILLING. It helps them move through the developmental process,
which is necessary in order to be successful. So willingness and
really being committed to the goal in the end really determines
whether or not a person is going to succeed. A person's goal is tied
to their belief system, and all of that, in my opinion, is largely—if
not completely—created by the way they were brought up.

I'll use myself as an example. The reason I made an entrepreneurial
decision at the age of five was that my parents were not involved in
my childhood. My dad did not come to my Little League games; I got
dropped off and picked up from Boy Scouts. My parents really were
not involved in what I was doing. So I taught myself that in order to
become worthy of attention and affection, to become worthy period,

I needed to produce something. My value and worth as an individual was based on how much I produced. Now I can look back and say that that is absolutely not true. But look at the limiting belief structure that this belief created in my life. It formed my entire basis—every belief, every construct, every decision I made was made through that lens of value. How do I become loved? Well, I have to create; I have to produce in order to be loved. It has nothing to do with my being loved—it has everything to do with what I am producing. I spent the vast majority of my life being driven by that fundamental belief system. Now, because of that, the likelihood of me quitting anything is very small because my entire context is based on not quitting. But you see, someone else could have a different belief structure where they quit everything.

RANDY: So how does someone develop that "thick skin" we are talking about? I've even heard it called a "rhino skin" where nothing will affect you. How does someone develop that?

STEVE: I wouldn't say I have thick skin, because I have worked really hard to disassemble that belief system. That belief system actually did not serve me well. If you look at my career path where I have made millions of dollars, most people would look at me and say, "Now that is a successful person." It _looked_ like I was successful: I have the big ranch in California, the stocks, the real estate, the money—but I have to tell you, I cried on my way to work every day. I was completely and horribly miserable every single day. I didn't have the life I thought I would have when I had all the money and had all the accolades. I was once recognized as one of the top turn-around, start-up guys in the Bay area. It was an honor. I achieved all the goals I had set out to do, but I hated my life. I was driven to continue. It wasn't until I left the technology world and

completed my first two years in network marketing
that I recognized that even though I left to have more time and more
financial freedom be with my family, even though I was successful
and making money in network marketing, I still wasn't happy. I
was still miserable. Where was this personal freedom? Why can't
I have this illusive time and financial freedom? Why can't I have
it, no matter what I do? Does this sound like a bazaar story to you,
Randy?

RANDY: No, not at all. Now, why do you think having money, fame,
and power doesn't satisfy completely?

STEVE: It doesn't satisfy, because that isn't what life is about.
Those things are what allow you to do other things. Having those
things empower you to do what really matters. If you are not focused
on what really matters, having money, fame, and power means
nothing.

RANDY: Absolutely. So as an entrepreneur, husband, and father,
how would you define success differently than our society defines
it?

STEVE: I define success now in terms of how much I give. Not
just financial giving, although it does include this. Pretty much, if I
invest myself in making other lives better, then I am successful. The
most successful day is when I have contributed in a way to someone
else's success.

RANDY: Philanthropy?

STEVE: Philanthropy is one way to describe it, or perhaps it is

just spending time with someone who needs some attention. We don't necessarily think of that as philanthropic, but for instance, someone came to me yesterday for a consultation. The discussion went a completely different way than we had scheduled it, but at the end of the day the person went away feeling like ten million bucks!

RANDY: What kind of lesson do you get from that?

STEVE: The lesson for me is that nothing else matters. It doesn't matter how many prospecting calls I make, how many executives I sign up, how much money I make. It doesn't matter. Remember, the belief system I was operating from was that my value is based on what I produce. So out of that framework, yesterday would have been a failure. I would have gone to bed thinking, "What a complete slug I am; I can't believe I wasted my time with that guy." Totally wrong!

RANDY: So you are saying abundance has more than a dollar title to it?

STEVE: Absolutely! Abundance has nothing to do with what I just said. Abundance has to do with me not even thinking about the money. The achievement, the amount I produce has nothing to do with abundant living. What I have learned is that achievement and abundance are disassociated; they are not connected at all. What I learned is that if I need money, I can pass the intention for money to the universe and say, "I intend to earn this much money this month," and then I don't need to give that another thought. From then on, I need to invest myself in other people. You know what happens? The money takes care of itself. I do some one-on-one coaching; I call

116

it breakthrough coaching. When I first enter into a dialogue with a client, money is part of that dialogue. People have commented that I don't seem too hung up on the money. Well, I'm not hung up on the money. The money has nothing to do with it. I want to earn so much money because I need the money. I mean, everyone needs money to pay the mortgage, buy gas, and buy food.

RANDY: Right, love makes the world go 'round, but money pays for the trip!

STEVE: That's a great way to say it! There is no association between me providing a client with a specific amount of coaching and a specific amount of money. This is something that was very hard for me to accept, coming from the belief system I was operating from. Then I realized that if I am providing value, the universe will reward me with the value I provide. Whether it comes from the client I am providing the service for or not, it doesn't matter. The important thing is that I get what I need because I am giving the value. So when I talk about a giving framework, it is really all about giving. You can call it philanthropic. I usually think of it as giving money to a cause.

My wife and I were actually just talking about this topic of giving. Can you really out give the universe? The answer is no. The universe just rewards us with more; the more we give, the more we get. We were talking about the things we wanted to buy, giving this and buying that. Wait a minute; buying is a form of giving, right? When I buy a car, someone is getting the money. So I am giving someone money, and what I am getting is a vehicle. So you shouldn't think in terms of "I shouldn't buy that because I should be giving my money to something else," because you are giving your money to something else. Buying is a form of giving. That doesn't mean we

shouldn't give to our church or other charities. If you are motivated to give, then give. At the same time, you don't want to put limitations on what to buy, because buying is also giving. Whether it is money, time, investing your energy, or quite frankly, praying for people, it's all giving.

RANDY: What happens when a leader doesn't take on this servant's attitude toward those they lead?

STEVE: Well, then they are not leading. If they are not serving, they are not leading. Leadership *is* service.

RANDY: I've found that most people get leadership confused with managing or being greedy. But if you are not serving, I guarantee you that you are not getting anything in return.

STEVE: If you are not serving, you are not leading. You know the old story: you can tell how strong a leader is by the number of people following him. How long is someone going to follow you if you are not investing in them? It isn't going to happen.

RANDY: Exactly. I have always believed in a team atmosphere. My buddy Mark Victor Hansen says it this way: TEAM stands for Together Everyone Achieves Miracles. Recently I have come up with something I call the Millionaire Mastermind Roundtable. I believe every successful person has had to overcome adversity, and I believe they have to have some type of system to overcome it. I believe successful people are now ready to teach the world abundance. We both believe that abundance is about way more than just money. It's about giving, it's about serving, and it's about leading with passion. I've discovered how important is it for someone to follow a

system of abundance, along with a tracking record,
to understand their progress. Basically, some people get discouraged right away; they don't understand that the process is really the pay off. They get into an organization for the payoff. The people you meet, the people you connect with—this is really the payoff.

STEVE: I was working with a gentleman on a coaching project. He gave me a sort of a mantra: "There is no destination; there is only a journey." Again, you can see how this is totally contradictory to the framework I had previously operated within. My whole life was set up as a destination. When I get there, I will do this. When I'm here, I can do this. When I've made this much money, I can go to Costa Rica. This is totally wrong, but that is how I did it. Now my life is set up as a journey. Part of my journey is to go to Costa Rica. The rest takes care of itself. To answer your question directly, you have to have a system. It is a journey, and there is a map. It doesn't mean you have to stay on the path you are on, but you do have to know which path you are on in order to enjoy the journey.

People frequently ask me, "How do I get from here to there?" Well, you don't. What you need to know is where here is and where there is. Everything else organizes itself. As long as you are on the path, you know you are moving forward. I like to help people look at progress in terms of accomplishments. Some of my coaches have assisted me to understand that the task orientation of the 80s and 90s simply breaks down in today's world. With the pace of information and processing and activities, we all have lots of irons in the fire. Truly successful people realize that you never really finish. You can't complete everything in a day, a week, a month, or a year. All you can do is continue to process, continue to advance, and continue to achieve and accomplish in incremental steps along your path to success.

RANDY: Mark Victor Hansen says that you never really retire. You just end up putting on a new set of wheels for the new journey ahead.

STEVE: That's right. Probably now more than any other time in history, people are going on multiple journeys in a single lifetime. You never arrive at anything. Retirement used to be a destination, which is why people went nuts when they got there, because now what did they do? Well, the context now is that there's no destination—life is a journey. If you are not enjoying the journey, then you've got it all wrong. You have to participate in the journey and be present with what is happening right now; you have to recognize and accept that right now everything around you is right exactly the way it should be. This is the perfect outcome for everything you have going on right now. Everything that has happened in your life has brought you to this particular moment in time. Guess what? The next moment in time is different because something else just happened. Once you begin to appreciate that, life begins to take on a more vibrant appeal. You can actually be present, stay present, and enjoy every instant for what it is, right now.

The way I manage my accomplishments in sort of an administrative way is that I document them. It may sound a little trivial, but I threw away my task list. I empower my day on my own, so the first item on my calendar might not be "Review your goals"—instead it might be a statement: "I have experienced the vision of my future." That may perhaps sound silly, but when I check that off my calendar, that is what I have accomplished. It is a slight difference, but what happens over time is you are so present during your day that you become increasingly more energized and elated until you are floating six inches off the ground! So when people say, "Hey, how are you

doing?" I can honestly say, "I am having the greatest day of my life!"

RANDY: Then they look at you and say, "What is wrong with you?" I usually say, "Outstanding!" People usually stand there for two to three seconds because they are in shock. It isn't your old run-of-the-mill answer of, "Oh, I'm doing fine" or "I'm okay." It's something different. Well, to stand out makes you outstanding.

STEVE: Someone asked me last night, "Hey, how are you today?" I told him, "Today is the greatest day of my life." He said, "Yeah, I heard you say that yesterday." So I replied, "Yesterday was the greatest day of my life yesterday, and today is the greatest day of my life today!" I say it just that way, and I FEEL that way! That's the truth, and it's the opposite of having a task destination framework that says, "I have to get this done, or I will never get to my destination. If I don't get to my destination, I have nothing to feel good about." To me, that is "heavy living." It's not vibrant, it's not fun, and it's not rewarding. It seems more like punishment. My thought pattern is, "This is ecstasy." Every minute of every day, I am exactly where I should be in that moment. Maybe it isn't what I thought of when I got up in the morning, but it's even better.

RANDY: So Steve, what do you think someone should do right now after reading this?

STEVE: I believe that action is the antidote to procrastination. People should put themselves in a quiet place and visualize what they want. They should visualize it exactly the way they want it with no regard for their limiting beliefs. If you say to yourself, "I intend to go to Costa Rica for thirty days—that is what I desire,"

and your instantaneous thought is, "Yeah, but I could never get off work that long," take the "Yeah, but..." out of there. Ask yourself, "What do I really want?" Write it down, make a recording of it, or perhaps find a picture of it. One of the most enjoyable moments of my life was when I took out my journal and described the home of my dreams in every detail, all the way down to the color of the tile. That visualization is what drove me, because I knew I was going to have that. I could see it, I could touch it, I knew it was there, and I was on my way to acquiring it. Every day I was that much closer to owning it. With that context, how could I ever be unhappy? It's important to start with visualization.

RANDY: Someone once asked Helen Keller, "Isn't it awful to lose your eyesight?" She said, "No…it's losing your vision." Vision is a powerful asset to anything you achieve, whether it's the man or woman of your dreams, a business venture you wish to pursue, or the lifestyle you long to achieve, or family you desire to have. Vision is very important.

STEVE: This is where people tend to get themselves into trouble. They do not accept vision in and of itself. They build their goal based on what they think they can do. When I train a new distributor in our organization, the first thing I always ask is "*Why* are you doing this business?"

Most people struggle with that answer at first because they are embarrassed about what they want. They tend to want one thing but say another. But what we ask them to tell us is what they REALLY want. However, the first answer is always what they think they can get. What they don't understand yet is that they can have anything they want. They just have to be able to visualize it, or it is impossible. The only thing keeping someone from achieving what they want to

achieve is their ability to see it.

RANDY: That's very, very powerful. Steve, I want to thank you so much for your time and sincerity. Thank you for being a part of my Millionaire Mastermind Roundtable group to teach wealth and abundance around the globe.

MILLIONAIRE MASTERMIND ROUNDTABLE

www.millionairepartnerships.com

Join us every Monday night at 7:30 p.m. PST for the Millionaire Mastermind Roundtable teleconference training call where Randy Gonzales, Jr. reveals the most effective, up-to-date strategies on enlightenment, wealth enhancement, inner healing, connecting from the heart, seven-figure results, millionaire techniques, self-esteem, and much more.

Allow Randy to teach you from the heart how to develop seven-figure results by being able to articulate your unique appeal so that the world's resources gravitate towards you. Randy will also have special guests periodically on the call. Be prepared to be instantly ready when opportunity comes knocking.

Every MONDAY at 7:30 p.m. PST
For Dial-In Number go to www.millionairepartnerships.com

Randy Gonzales, Jr.
www.millionairepartnerships.com

"MAX OUT your self-help and personal development from these teachings. LISTEN to Randy!"

Mark Victor-Hansen, *cocreator of the Chicken Soup for the Soul series*

www.millionairepartnerships.com

Books:
The Unbreakable Human Spirit Series:

  Coming Soon:
The Unbreakable Human Spirit for Network Marketers
The Unbreakable Human Spirit for Women Entrepreneurs
The Unbreakable Human Spirit for Mothers
The Unbreakable Human Spirit for Investors
The Unbreakable Human Spirit for Couples

Audio:
Within My Reach 8-CD Set
How to Play

Within My Reach 2-CD Set
Practical Actions of a Millionaire

Set in Motion CD
48 Hours to Liftoff

Affirmation Cards
52 Enlightened Weeks of Abundance

Results Coaching:

Seeking Peak Performance?

Randy Gonzales, Jr. has developed one-on-one mentoring for individuals seeking abundance, growth, and prosperity. He specializes in assisting people to take one hundred percent full responsibility for their lives. Randy understands that great moments are born from great opportunities. Every adversity you face is another great moment in your life waiting to be born. Let Randy assist you to evolve from where you are to where you desire to be.

www.millionairerolodex.com

One of the most important words in the English language isn't in the dictionary. It's "Rolodex." Your network is directly proportional to your net worth. S.O.C. is an innovative operation that allows you to generate a successful network by the click of a button. I've always considered myself a student of the game. Anytime I come across an intriguing business book, a good article, the latest CD, or any other tool, I experiment with it, and then based upon my result, I put it into my arsenal of effective networking. From the vantage point of my fourteen-year networking career, here's why I see S.O.C. as a must:

- *Imagine a system that will never let you forget a birthday again.*
- *Imagine a way to send an unexpected card every day to people you care about.*
- *Imagine the ability to act on an inner prompting and express yourself to someone who needs it.*
- *Imagine following up with customers, clients, and prospects in less than sixty seconds.*

Do you believe that relaying a simple act of kindness could create a huge difference? You bet!

An ancient Chinese proverb advises:
If you want one year of prosperity, grow grains.
If you want ten years of prosperity, grow trees.
If you want one hundred years of prosperity, grow people.

If you send me an e-mail with "I want a free gift account" in the subject line, I will give you a **FREE** *gift account so you can experience what I have experienced with this system. E-mail me at soc@ millionairepartnerships.com. Send me your name, phone number, e-mail, and the best time to reach you so either myself or one of my staff can give you a quick walk-through on how to set up your* **FREE** *account. And watch how you too will develop a multimillion-dollar rolodex! E-mail me* **now** *for your free account.*

BOOK WISE

& COMPANY

The lessons of a lifetime can be transferred from an author's mind to yours in a few short hours, saving you time and money. Books are transformational. Books are powerful. They contain the condensed wisdom and skill of the smartest minds in the world. Books give you leverage.

You'll know what we mean when we say that the right book at the right time is literally worth its weight in gold. I believe in lifelong learning. The books we read accomplish for our minds what exercise does for our bodies.

BookWise & Company is the next revolution in the book world: the newest chapter in the ever-changing business of books. The twenty-four-billion-dollar book industry has never been stronger. BookWise offers the ability to increase literacy and personal growth, while providing an unparalleled opportunity for entrepreneurs. For more information on BookWise, visit:

www.mastermindthinking.com